The Alexamenos Graffito

THE ALEXAMENOS GRAFFITO

An Early Roman Commentary on Christians and Christianity

Thomas R. Young

RESOURCE *Publications* • Eugene, Oregon

THE ALEXAMENOS GRAFFITO
An Early Roman Commentary on Christians and Christianity

Resource Publications
An Imprint of Wipf and Stock Publishers
199 W. 8th Ave., Suite 3
Eugene, OR 97401

www.wipfandstock.com

PAPERBACK ISBN: 979-8-3852-1693-2
HARDCOVER ISBN: 979-8-3852-1694-9
EBOOK ISBN: 979-8-3852-1695-6

VERSION NUMBER 01/29/25

To Kim, Sarah and Henry

The Alexamenos Grafitto
Rodolpho Lanciani/ Public Domain

Contents

CONTENTS

List of Illustrations

Photographs and Illustrations by the Author
or in the Public Domain

Introduction

SINCE ITS DISCOVERY IN 1857 in a room of the Pedagogium, a one-time imperial palace turned page school on the Palatine Hill in Rome, the Alexamenos Graffito has been one of the most widely known inscriptions attributed to early Roman attitudes toward Christianity. Early after its discovery, the Graffito was described and interpreted by an international host of nineteenth century writers and scholars. These individuals provided descriptions of the physical layout of the Pedagogium where the artifact was found, speculated on the date of the inscription, its interpretation, and generally commented on other graffiti that otherwise appeared on the Pedagogium's plaster walls. This early commentary, written by English, Italian, and German authorities, was scholarly but in many cases served a primary purpose to serve as fodder to fill guidebooks for the wealthy as they made their way through the then eponymous "Grand Tour" of Europe.

For the most part, the late nineteenth and early twentieth century and writing about the Alexamenos Graffito, with a few exceptions, reached the same conclusion about the Graffito's meaning and purpose, namely that the Graffito was a blasphemous representation of Jesus of Nazareth on the cross. To the extent that such a conclusion was correct, the Graffito served mainly as a reminder of early Roman attitudes toward Christians, and confirmed the opinions of Christian Apologists like Tertullian,

Lactantius, and Eusebius, who also noted the callous regard many Romans had for Christians and Christianity.

This work examines the work of previous scholarship and seeks to expand upon the somewhat summary conclusions of those who have examined the Graffito. In doing so, this work advances the claim that the Alexamenos Graffito is much more than just another example of anti-Christian propaganda. Rather, the Graffito will be shown to be an important artifact of material culture which helps us to understand the attitudes and beliefs held not by the educated elite, for which we have abundant evidence, but rather the far rarer voice of ordinary individuals from the lower social strata of Roman society in the second and third centuries. Unlike the Senatorial Class authorities who have famously commented upon Christianity like Tacitus, Celsus, and Pliny the Younger, the author of the Graffito, perhaps an imperial page or a slave, provides the modern reader with the sentiments of a solitary individual with little political power and likely even less social standing.

Secondly, it will be argued that this rare voice of a common individual provides a modern audience considerable insight about Christianity's reach into Roman society. For example, the Graffito's text and imagery suggest that the author of the Graffito's attitudes and beliefs were ill-informed about the difference between Judaism and Christianity. A notable example of this is the Graffito author's portrayal of Jesus of Nazareth as a god with the head of an ass. Such a portrayal had also noted by the second century North African Christian apologists Tertullian and Municius Felix in the Roman Province of Africa Proconsularis. This correlation of erroneous belief strongly suggests the possibility that the author's contact with Christians may have been irregular and the particular beliefs expressed about Christians might have been objectively held by other non-elites of society.

Beyond the implications the Graffito has for the author's understanding of Christianity and Judaism, the Grafitto also betrays the author's subjective attitude toward Christians. In this it differs greatly with known elite opinions which often exhibited a deep conservatism which was openly hostile toward religious practices that deviated from traditional cult worship, whether that was the state-prescribed public cult or private cult worship that took place in individual households. This elite opinion toward deviant cultic practices, carried on well beyond mere polemics and probably was responsible for acts of state persecution. The persecution of the practitioners of Bacchic worship and those dedicated to the worship of Isis are notable examples of this. Quite contrary to known elite opinion, the Alexamenos Graffito shows nothing of the overt animus often found in some of the more elite critiques, which charge Christians with atheism, superstition, and even cannibalism.

Finally, this work examines how the Alexamenos Grafitto informs modern scholarhip about Roman civilization at the time of work's creation. Not only does the Grafitto provide visual clues about cultic practices but also about Roman justice, Roman attire; as well as lingual and demographic information telling about the languages spoken and written as well as the probable origins of those involved in such communication.

With these points in mind, this work seeks to explore the Alexamenos Graffito in a more comprehensive way than has been undertaken thus far by prior scholarship. This undertaking is accomplished sequentially and step by step, first of all, through a thorough investigation of the Graffito's social, cultural, literary, and religious background. Next, the archaeological context in which the Graffito was created is explored, from the archaeology of the City of Rome and the Palatine Hill to the particulars that relate to the Pedagogium, where the Alexamenos Graffito was originally located. This work will then consider the Graffito's discourse, the interpretation of that discourse, and will finally seek to explicate those conclusions referenced above about the Graffito as it relates to the larger conversation going on in the first through third centuries about the place of Christianity as well as other non-native religions that had reached Roman soil.

To accomplish its aims, this work is organized by chapters which take a broad brush approach to setting the social, cultural, religious, and architectural context for the Graffito before settling down to the particular details of the work. Chapter One seeks to set forth the definitions used and to carry out the exploration of the Grafitto and its religious and cultural context. Chapter Two provides the reader a brief narrative of Christian History and Christianity's place within the Roman Empire in the first through third centuries. The Third Chapter examines broadly traditional Roman cult, both public and private, while the fourth chapter examines the parameters of Roman intolerance of non-native cult and religious practices.

With the Fifth Chapter, the work leaves the realm of providing social and cultural context and begins to consider with great particularity the physical context in which the Graffito was found as it relates to the city of Rome, the Palatine Hill situated within the city itself, and the particular structures most identifiable with the Graffito, the Domus Augustiana and the Pedagogium. Chapter Six entertains an analysis of the particular components of the Graffito, analyzing each element of its pictorial and textual discourse and developing the social and cultural implications of each. Finally, the Seventh Chapter sums up the particular findings related to the Graffito and seeks to integrate these findings into the overall picture of current scholarship as it relates to the intersection between the traditional Roman cult practitioners and the more recent and increasingly numerous Christians.

—— PART ONE ——

PROGLEMENA

CHAPTER ONE

Definitions and Clarifications

IN CLASSICAL AND RELIGIOUS Studies it is critical to adequately define terms. This is to assure that the reader understands the ambiguities and nuances contained in those terms when used to describe the ritual practices, sacrificial acts, worship, and veneration of non-Christian peoples. This work employs the tools and methods of comparative religion to explore the interplay between practitioners of early Christianity and those who practiced traditional Roman cultic activities in the first through third centuries. The use of such tools comes with a price in that comparative methodology employs the use of a vocabulary of a known religion (i.e. Christianity) to describe the cultic practices of the Roman people. In doing so, there is, as a byproduct, a suggestion of affinity and similarity between Christians and the traditional practitioners of Roman cult which was largely not actually present. Accordingly, this chapter seeks to define a number of the terms used and provide an abundance of clarification to enable the reader to take a cautious approach when considering the implications of certain key terms and phrases used in this work.

Roman

This work utilizes the word "Roman" liberally when describing religious practices to include reference to both those practices of the people of the City of Rome as well as to people outside the City and even outside the Italian Peninsula. There is a degree of truth to the notion that in many places where the Romans went, whether trading or conquering, they spread their culture and in many cases, this culture bore significant fruit replicating itself in places far from the culture's origin. However, this concept of "romanization" where Roman culture and cultural practices became something analogous to an invasive species, taking over and dominating the lands and peoples the Romans came into contact with, has been the subject of controversy for a number of decades has precarious credibility.[1] As it relates to religion, the concept of romanization is troubled by the presumption that the gods worshiped by the Romans were purely of domestic origin. To the contrary, there is strong evidence to suggest that many so-called Roman domestic gods may have had Etruscan, Punic, or Greek origins.[2] Secondly, the religious practices of the Roman people differed decidedly by geography. For example, in the port city of Ostia which is under twenty miles to the west of Rome, the Capitoline triad of Jupiter Optimus Maximus, Juno, and Minerva were worshiped the same as they were in Rome. So too were the gods Castor and Pollux,

---

1. See e.g. Greg Woolf, "Beyond Romans and Natives," *World Archaeology* 28 (3) (1995), 339-350, which argues that rather than bringing about homogenization and cultural convergence in the Roman Province of Gaul, Roman imperialism actually created new kinds of social class and regional differences and that rather than be assimilated, the people of Gaul were participants in the creation of a new social order; See also Elizabeth Fentress, "Romanizing the Berbers," *Past & Present* 190. (Feb. 2006), 3-33. which argues that Roman imperialism in North Africa liberated individuals from family and clan restrictions and shifted property from commonly held property toward individual accumulation of landed property, thus empowering the individual rather than make him involuntarily subject to impersonal imperial forces.

2. Michael Grant, *The Etruscans* (New York: Quality Paperbacks, 1997), 151-153; Jorg Rupke, *Religion of the Romans* (Cambridge: Polity Press, 2007), 51-61.

Venus, Fortuna, Ceres, and Hercules worshiped in both munici-palities.[3] However, unique to Ostia was at least one geographically unique cult, that of the cult of the Genius of the Colony of Os-tia (*Genius Coloniae Ostensium*) which provided for the worship of divine (as opposed to the mere physical) nature of the City.[4] Even more striking evidence of geographical diversity in religious worship can be identified from the archeological findings from the fortress towns along Hadrian's Wall in the Roman Province of Britannia. There one finds, along with eponymous worship of the Unconquerable Sun (*Sol Invicto*), Jupiter Optimus Maximus, Fortuna, Mithras, and Apollo, cult objects and statuary dedicated to the Celtic god Maponus, and the German goddesses Harimella, Ricagambeda, and Virodechtis, none of which are to be found in the City of Rome.[5] Accordingly, when Roman religious practices are mentioned in this text, the reader should keep in mind that while many of the gods worshiped utilized similar rituals, there was no absolute homogeneity with respect to the pantheon of gods worshiped throughout territory controlled by Rome. The word "Roman" should, therefore, be construed as a loose term that ap-plies generally to the cultic practices of peoples under Roman rule or, more particularly, to the private and public cultic practices in the City of Rome itself. Therefore, context is important in deter-mining in which way the term is being used.

Religion

The use of the term religion is problematic when considering the particular practices of the Romans in worshiping and venerating their gods. Outside of the context of Roman culture and history, ef-forts at defining the term have been elusive. That elusiveness, how-ever, has not prevented a host of notable efforts to find a workable

3. See generally, L. Ross Taylor, *The Cults of Ostia* (Chicago: Ares Publish-ing, 1913).

4. See generally, Taylor, *The Cults of Ostia*.

5. Ronald Embleton and Frank Graham. *Hadrian's Wall* (New York: Dorset Press, 1984), 273.

and robust definition. The early twentieth century English scholar James Frazer tried to encapsulate the essence of religion as "belief in powers higher than man and an attempt to propitiate or please them."[6] Emile Durkheim, a pioneer in the sociological study of religion, defined religion as a ". . . unified system of beliefs and practices relative to sacred things, that is to say, things set apart and forbidden-beliefs and practices which unite into one single moral community called a Church, all those who adhere to them."[7] Obviously, the deficiencies in each of these definitions have made them less than satisfactory when trying to apply the wide variety of rites, rituals, and practices which seem religious in nature but lack exist independently of the commands and admonitions of a divine being or where there is no requisite organized community for which these rites, rituals and practices are restricted.

Perhaps one of the more bold, if not altogether successful, efforts to define religion has arisen as a result of the sociological research of the American anthropologist Clifford Geertz (1926-2006) who defined religion as "(1) a system of symbols which acts to (2) establish powerful, pervasive, and long lasting moods and motivations in men by (3) formulating conceptions of a general order of existence and (4) clothing these conceptions with such an aura of factuality that (5) the moods and motivations seem uniquely realistic."[8] This definition has a number of advantages, not the least of which is that it seeks to provide a universal definition of all symbolic systems and ritual practices through wider interpretation of the work already undertaken by such earlier theorists as Emile Durkheim, Max Weber, and members of the British School of Anthropology, including Bronislaw Malinowski (1884-1942);

6. James George Frazer. *The Golden Bough* (New York: Collier/Macmillan, 1922), 58.

7. Emile Durkheim. *The Elementary Forms of Religious Life*, trans. Joseph Ward Swain (New York: Freepress/MacMillan, 1915), 62.

8. Clifford Geertz. *The Interpretation of Cultures* (San Francisco: Basic Books, 1973), 88; Ashley Leibner, "The Anthropology of Religion: Historical and Contemporary Trends," in *Macmillan Handbooks on Religion: Historical Consciousness and the Social Sciences*. ed. William B. Parsons (London: Palgrave Macmillan, 2016), 241-247.

Alfred Reginald Ratcliff-Brown (1881-1951); E.E. Evans-Pritchard (1902-1973) and Godfrey Lienhardt (1921-1993). The robustness of Geertz definition has, despite its usefulness, come under attack by scholars who find the definition rooted in a particular historical period coinciding with Christian domination in Europe and the power it employed in perpetuating a particular understanding of the world. For example, Talal Asad, in his critique of Geertz' definition of religion highlights Geertz' employment of the anthropological techniques of translation where our everyday language is used to "convey the coherence of other ways of life, thought ,and communication."[9] The problem with such techniques, according to Assad, is that there is not universal equivalency between the use of symbols or ritual practices between cultures. Furthermore, certain concepts, such as the concept of belief, may not even be found in the language of certain peoples or cultures which engaging in such symbolic use or ritualistic practices.[10]

With such reservations in mind about giving proper definition to the term, "religion" will be used sparingly and when used at all will largely be to describe Christian practices. This will assist in avoiding false translation of traditional Roman cultic practices and assist the reader in understanding their function without having to assign them to a category or classification that is more congruous with the practices of Christians. When describing the ritual, sacrifice, and devotional practices of the non-Christian, Roman people, more often than not use will be made of the term "Roman cult".

9. See e.g. Talal Asad., "Anthropological Conceptions of Religion: Reflections on Geertz." *Man, New Series* 18(2) (1983), 237. For other criticism, see generally Ashley Leibner, *The Anthropology of Religion: Historical and Contemporary Trends* in *Macmillan Handbooks on Religion: Historical Consciousness and the Social Sciences.* ed. William B. Parsons (London: Palgrave Macmillan, 2016).

10. Leibner, *Anthropology of Religion,* 241.

Roman Private or Domestic Cult

References to Private or Domestic Cult are meant, at minimum, those privately financed acts of the Romans of prayer, devotion, ritual, and sacrifice which took place in a domestic setting and that were presided over by the male head of the household (*paterfamilias*). This definition borrows heavily from Pompeius Festus and Cicero, both of whom, in the second century of the Common Era, helped to differentiate domestic cult from the public cult maintained by the Roman State.[11] For the purposes of further definition, the household meant not only the head of the household (*paterfamilias*) and his immediate family but also all others who resided in a single house (*domus*) including slaves, freedmen, and freeborn kin.[12] Unlike either the definitions of domestic cult formulated by either Pompeius Festus or Cicero, which restricted the gods worshiped domestically to those publicly accepted or those worshiped by one's ancestors, domestic cult as defined by this work recognizes the liberality employed by the paterfamilias in selecting the gods that were worshiped by the household. Traditionally, domestic cult included in its veneration and worship two classes of household gods: the *Lares*, or generic entities who offered protection to those who sought their assistance, and the *Penates*, or ancestral gods attached to a family that provided such protection as well. However, aside from these two classes, households often included worship of other gods as well, including those from the public cult as well as others chosen by the paterfamilias.[13] Thus, such an "intermingling of deities" from

11. John Bodel, "Cicero's Minerva, Penates, and the Mother of the Lares: An Outline of Roman Domestic Religion" in *Household and Family Religion in Antiquity*. ed. John Bodel and Saul M. Olyan. (Oxford: Blackwell, 2008), 249-250.

12. Bodel, "Cicero's Minerva, Penates, and the Mother of the Lares," 250-251.

13. For example, in addition to the other gods worshiped in his household, Cicero also worshiped the public cult god Minerva, whose statue he rescued from his home and dedicated to the city of Rome. See Bodel, "Cicero's Minerva, Penates, and the Mother of the Lares," 255; Cicero, *De Legibus*. 2.42

both the public and domestic sphere was not an uncommon characteristic of Roman domestic religious practice.[14]

Roman Public Cult

Roman public or State cult will always mean those rituals, sacrificial acts, acts of divination and augury, worship and veneration conducted at State expense or through private financing arranged by the State and undertaken by professionals paid for by the Roman State.[15] As alluded to before, the reader should be aware that while the Roman State might finance the afore-mentioned activities throughout territories under Roman control, the actual deities worshiped would vary by geography, with most nearly all regions engaging in worship of a core list of deities (i.e. Jupiter, Juno and Minerva) but would also pay tribute to local or ethnic gods unique to geographic location.

Sources

No work seeking to discuss the history of ancient Rome should neglect to discus the source basis for knowledge of this history. Remarkably, after a little less than two thousand years, there is quite an extensive literary record and body of material culture upon which facts about the Roman Republic and Empire can be gleaned. However, there are problems of utility regarding the available resources available to the historian of Rome, however abundant those resources may be. With regard to the literary record, there are excellent histories from the likes of Polybius, Livy, Caesar, Tacitus, and Ammianus Marcellinus, among others. However, in some cases, the histories of these authors are in some cases incomplete, with books missing or corrupted, leaving gaps in the narrative. Further, some of these sources relied upon other authorities, which is not a problem if the source historian got the facts right but a big problem

---

14. Bodel, "Cicero's Minerva, Penates, and the Mother of the Lares," 251
15. Bodel, "Cicero's Minerva, Penates, and the Mother of the Lares," 249.

if not, especially when many of the surviving works were written at some distance in time from the events narrated. Finally, there is the problem that most of the histories that survive were written by male Roman elites of the Senatorial or Equestrian Classes and express the viewpoints and biases associated with the same, leaving the perspectives of the lower class Plebeians, freedmen, slaves and women unexpressed and providing little to no basis for gaining insight into their lives and experiences.

These same problems are less evident with respect to the material culture bequeathed by the Roman Republic and Empire to the present day. A great deal of material culture, from public and private buildings to inscriptions, letters, weapons, armor, clothing, preserved food, and even the remains of human parasites from the Roman people, still exists and are available to provide raw historical data for the researcher. Furthermore, unlike Roman literary resources, the surviving material culture of the Republic and Empire tends to be much more democratic in terms of the sources from which it originated, whether it be the public inscriptions on buildings placed there by public officials, the letter by a lonely soldier to the folks back home recovered from a trash dump on the Roman frontier, painted frescoes on the walls of a Senator's Pompeian villa, or fecal deposits recovered from a city cistern containing food scraps and the casings of desiccated worms In most cases, the evidence comes from a variety of classes and transcends geographical boundaries and portrays more robustly the actual material conditions that existed in a now gone Roman world. However, with such benefits that come from the use of material culture come also a few detriments. First among these is the fact that material culture doesn't always tell its story in a linear fashion. A prime example can be found in the ancient North African city of Thugga. While the city preserves many examples of extant temple architecture, public baths, private residences, triumphal archways, statuary, and mosaics, a visitor today would see not Thugga as it appeared as a prosperous and orderly agricultural center of the second century but rather a bastion hastily constructed of any stone building material that was at hand thrown together willy-nilly into a defensive structure by the armies of Justinian in the fourth century. In essence, these troops quarried and repurposed existing structural material to build something new to meet the needs of the time, thereby distorting the historical record. This same condition exists throughout the empire, from the City of Rome to the far reaches of Hadrian's Wall in the then existing Roman province of Brittania.

Accordingly, this work makes use of Roman literary sources freely but with the understanding that these same sources suffer from serious defects in terms of the their authority and their ability to represent the diverse peoples and classes of the Roman Republic and Empire. Wherever possible, resort is made to material culture in an effort to broaden the likelihood that an accurate picture is portrayed. However, the author is likewise well aware of the limitations of material culture and recognizes the potential for factual distortion in this area as well.

Aside from the Roman sources, this work makes use extensively of late nineteenth century scholarship regarding the Alexamenos Graffito, the Domus Gelantiana and Domus Augustana to describe the physical geography and contents of the these objects and spaces. The reason for this is simply due to the fact that most of the objects and spaces identified in this work no longer are in their original context, have been severely degraded, vandalized, or simply no longer exist. These nineteenth century scholars are oftentimes the last credible witnesses we have of what was and is no longer available for inspection. While there is danger in taking their observations and conclusions at face value, the abundant quantity of such commentators provides some ability to triangulate facts and observations. Accordingly, this work will drink deeply from the words of Marucci, Lanciani, Hogg, Middleton, and others when setting the scene of what once was.

Elites and Non-Elites

Roman society was a very stratified society divided by status. Status could be seen broadly in the stratification of wealth in antiquity, which was, as it is the present, the product of one's ability to access and control capital: those who had the least ability to possess or control capital generally appeared at the bottom economic wrung of society while those with more access generally occupied higher strata. Slaves often occupied the lowest economic position due to their subjugation to their owner who could, if the owner chose, confiscate all of the slave's possessions. However, many slaves were treated as equals by their owners, were entrusted with important responsibilities involving financial management, and upon their owners death, were often rewarded with both their freedom and a liberal inheritance.[16]

On the other hand, those of the Senatorial Class, which required property worth approximately one million sesterces (one sesterce equally approximately $6-$7 U.S. dollars) for membership in the elite class, were largely at the top economic position, despite the fact that senatorial class citizens were prohibited by law and custom from engaging in industry and commerce.[17] This problem was overcome through ownership in land. Individuals at the economic summit of Roman society often had abundant landholdings in their portfolio of assets which often underpinned the fortunes of not only the rural aristocracy but often the urban aristocracy as well who frequently, along with their urban dwellings, owned estates and villas in the countryside.[18]

Between the slaves and the Senators were other classes as well, beginning with former slaves, or Freedmen. Despite their start at a lower economic position, Freedmen often demonstrated that economic stratification was by no means monolithic. Indeed, one of the more celebrated tales of Roman literature of that of Petronious' *Satyricon*, which includes a sumptuous dinner provided to clients by Tramalchio, a now rich freedman who, as a slave,

16. Samuel Dill, *Roman Society from Nero to Marcus Aurelius* (New York: Meridian, 1954), 102.

17. Dill, *Roman Society from Nero to Marcus Aurelius,* 102; Daisy Dunn, *The Shadow of Vesuvius: A Life of Pliny* (London: Norton, 2019), 20. By comparison, a common laborer could expect to earn 1000 sesterces in a year.

18. David Mattingly, *An Imperial Possession: Britain and the Roman Empire* (London: Penguin Books 2007), 453.

occupied the lowest echelons of economic society.[19] At or slightly above Freedmen were the those of the proletariat and mercantile class who engaged in small scale farming and advanced many trades that made Roman society possible.

Finally, status could also be conferred by political patronage. In the provinces annexed by Rome following military conquest, very often provincial elites who offered their loyalty to the Roman conquerors could expect assistance in consolidating landholdings or in other areas that would enhance the provincial's prestige.[20]

A high status was essential to an individual becoming a cultural elite. Those with wealth had greater opportunity to be educated, and had greater expectations placed by society to participate in societal culture.

Those with low status, conversely, often had nothing but the most basic education (if any education at all) and were at best passive observers of the cultural world that surrounded them.

As a result, literature and art tended to be the product of those, due their wealth and position, who had the ability to write and create. Those who did not very often were at pains to merely survive. Accordingly, nearly all the extant literature from Rome comes from elites and very little from non-elites has been transmitted to the present era. Rather, to glean any understanding of the thoughts and circumstances of the non-elites, resort must be made to material culture such as funerary inscriptions, graffiti, preserved letters and documents, and preserved artifacts which by good fortune came to be discovered through archeology.

19. See generally Petronius, *The Satyricon*, trans. J.P. Sullivan (London: Penguin, 1986).

20. Mattingly, *Imperial Possession*, 454.

CHAPTER TWO

A Brief Survey of Early Christianity

The Religion of "Christus"

CHRISTIANITY BEGAN AS A social and religious movement centered around the teachings and mission of Jesus of Nazareth in the first century of the Common Era. Born in approximately 7 to 4 BCE, during the last years of Herod the Great, client king of Judea, Jesus was a teacher and religious reformer who claimed a special authority and relationship with the Judaic God.[1] His message, preached almost exclusively to the Jews, was both traditional and radical, speaking in a way rooted to the native soil of Palestine and venerating traditional Judaism yet waging war " . . against the selfish, self righteous temper" of many of the Jewish religious leaders and attacking Jewish arrogance that by " . . virtue of their descent, [the Jews] were sure of salvation."[2] Likewise, Jesus preached to all who would hear recurring themes of the "the good news" of salvation from the grave, promising eternal life to believers and eternal damnation who rejected the words he spoke. To help promulgate this eschatological message, Jesus assembled around him twelve

1. L. Michael White, *Scripting Jesus* (New York: HarperOne, 2010), 5; William C. Placher, *A History of Christian Theology* (Louisville, KY: Westminster John Knox, 1983), 29-30.

2. Adolf Harnack. *The Mission and Expansion of Christianity*, Translated by James Moffatt (New York: Harper Brothers, 1961), 36.

disciples. While little is known about the backgrounds of those individuals chosen by Jesus, there is authority to suggest that the disciple Peter, his brother, Andrew; James, and his brother, John, were fishermen who worked vessels on the Sea of Galilee.[3] Likewise, the disciple Matthew is reputed to have earned his living as a private tax farmer, a position largely reviled in Roman society for the methods employed to collect taxes for the Emperor and the Roman State.[4] Finally, while his occupation is unknown, the disciple Simon was described as being a member of the Zealots, a group who identified with Judas the Galilean, founder of the "fourth philosophy" of the Jews, and who later became an element of resistance against Roman rule at the fortress of Masada in 66 CE.[5] Thus, Jesus' disciples and his other followers, which included individuals from all walks of life and also included a number of women, were a fairly diverse group.

Jesus' message of redemption and repentance was brought to the people of Palestine, first in Lower Galilee, then to Jerusalem. Along with his preaching, Jesus also performed many acts attributed to be miracles such as healing the blind, lame, sick and infirm and even resurrecting the dead.[6] Such undertakings were at the time often attributable to persons who practiced "magic" and "sorcery" which, under Roman Law, was subject to capital punishment.[7] Further, Jesus engaged in the practice of exorcism, casting out demons on several occasions, which further exposed Jesus (and his disciples who exorcized demons in Jesus' name) to charges of being a magician.[8] It was in Jerusalem that Jesus'

3. Matthew 4:18-22; Matthew 10:3.

4. J. Lane Miller, *Harper's Bible Dictionary* (New York: Harper and Brothers, 1961), 427.

5. Jack Finegan, *The Archeology of the New Testament* (Princeton, New Jersey: Princeton University Press 1992), 27.

6. John 4:43-54; Mathew 8:14-15; Mathew 8:16-17; Matthew 9:1-8; Luke 7:11-17.

7. Robert L. Wilken, *The Christians as the Romans Saw Them* (New Haven: Yale University Press, 1984), 99; Justin Meggitt, "Did Magic Matter? The Saliency of Magic in the Early Roman Empire" *Journal of Ancient History* 1, 2 (2013): 173-174.

8. Wilken, *Christians as the Romans Saw Them*, 99.

ministry came to an end outside the walls of Jerusalem between 26-30 CE with his crucifixion at the hands of the Jewish priestly central authority, the Sanhedron, and the Roman Prefect, Pontias Pilate, who acquiesced to the Sanhedron's death sentence upon Jesus for blasphemy.[9] As a type of punishment, crucifixion existed as a general category of punishment by suspension and may have involved a particular device of torture, such as being physically secured to a board or beams.[10]

Jesus of Nazareth

Inverness, Scotland/Photo by Author

9. White, *Scripting Jesus,* 5.

10. Felicity Harley "Crucifixion in Roman Antiquity: The State of the Field," *Journal of Early Christian Studies* 27. 2 (Summer 2019): 303-323, 311-317.

Crucifixion, as practiced by the Romans, was usually reserved for slaves and criminals.[11] Thanks to Alexander the Great, who preferred this form of execution to other available options, crucifixion was rather ubiquitous in the Mediterranean. At the time Jesus was condemned by the Sanhedron, Alexander's methods had become his successor's methods and crucifixion, with modifications, remained in constant use.[12] These modifications included the choice of beams used to affix the person being crucified and, at least by the time of the Romans, included flogging and securing the victim by the use of a single bolt or nail driven into both feet.[13] That such a form of punishment was used on Jesus is hardly surprising given Jesus' attacks against the Jewish religious hierarchy and the disruptive effect his ministry had in volatile Palestine, a fact that could hardly have been ignored by Roman authorities.

Jesus' death in an ancient world, where life was frequently cheap, did not go unnoticed. This was partly due to the many diverse implications Jesus' life had for so many people. To Jesus' disciples and to an increasing number of Jews and non-Jews, Jesus was the Messiah, the redeemer of Israel, whose coming had been foretold by the Hebrew Prophets, and whose destiny was to overthrow the Roman oppressors and restore the once proud kingdom to its former glory in the days of King Solomon. To other Jews, Jesus represented a malignant presence, a blasphemer, and a menace to the established religious order whose constant challenges required the most aggressive campaign of repression. Finally to the Romans, Jesus was viewed as just another dangerous fanatic (whom the second century Roman Historian Tacitus mislabeled "Christus") who challenged their political authority and with it, the legitimacy of the Roman State.[14]

Shortly following Jesus death, a second phase of Jesus' ministry began: the worldwide expansion of what would be known as the Christian faith. As one scholar has commented, "the death

11. Harley, "Crucifixion in Roman Antiquity," 303-323, 311-317.
12. Brian Moynihan, *The Faith* (New York: Doubleday, 2002), 14.
13. Moynihan, *Faith*, 4.
14. Tacitus, *Annals* 15.44.

[of Jesus] was more effective than his life; it failed to shatter faith in him as one sent by God, and hence the conviction of his resurrection arose."[15] With theological origins rooted in Judaism, cultural origins with the Jewish people, and geographical and cultural moorings in the Roman provinces of Syria and Judaea, the adherents of the early Christian mission were initially perceived as belonging to yet another Judaic sect like the Pharisees, Sadducees, and the Essenes.[16] The reason for this perception was multi-faceted. First of all, such a view was a reasonable inference given that the geographical infrastructure of the early Church very often mirrored the network of synagogues spread throughout the Roman Empire as a result of the Diaspora.[17] Secondly, this perception was reinforced by the fact that the members of the earliest Christians congregations were often drawn from the Jewish population of Syria and Judaea so that, by mid-way into the first century of the Common Era, there were substantial enclaves of Christian Jews in the capital of Jerusalem as well as in rural Judea and north into the region of Galilee.[18] This misperception inevitably began to expand in scope with the advent of the missionary activity of the Christians in Antioch, who sought to extend the Christian message to the Greeks in that city, as well as the evangelical activity of Paul and Barnabas, who extended the mission of conversion to Syria and Cilicia before moving on to other parts of the Roman Empire.[19] Building on this foothold, Christianity was later able to branch out into other non-Jewish populations, including those found in Cappadocia, Galatia, Pontus, Thracia, Macedonia, and Dalmatia, and into the Italic peninsula itself.[20]

With the shift from a largely Judaic-oriented Christianity to one which more widely was composed of both Jews and gentiles,

15. Harnack, *Mission and Expansion of Christianity*, 44.

16. Henry Chadwick, *The Early Church* (London: Penguin, 1990), 13.

17. Chadwick, *Early Church*, 15-16.

18. Chadwick, *Early Church*, 15-16.; Harnack. at 1; 15.

19. Chadwick, *Early Church*, 16; Diarmaid MacCulloch, *Christianity: The First Three Thousand Years* (New York: Viking, 2009), 109

20. Harnack, *Mission and Expansion of Christianity*, xx-xxi.

the barriers to entry into communion with the early Christian communities were significantly reduced. Furthermore, with missionary activities increasingly focusing on both the rural villages of Palestine to the major Graeco-Roman cities of the Mediterranean, Christianity was able to reach increasing numbers of people who, unlike those in the more conservative rural hinterland, were more acclimatized to new ideas and change.[21] Predictably, the numbers of those in the Roman Empire increased to such a degree that the chance that a person in the Roman Empire would encounter a Christian became an increasing likelihood, particularly after the second century of the Common Era.[22] The increased mobility of many people within the empire during this period, attributable to the protection of land and sea afforded travelers by the Roman authorities, as well as by the vast network of roads developed throughout the empire, also contributed to the increased likelihood of contact between Christians and non-Christians.[23]

With increased contact came increased conflict. This conflict manifested itself in two ways: first, through conflict between Christians and non-Christians, and secondly, between differing sects that began to form within Christianity. Regarding the first source of conflict, discord notably arose between Jews and Christians when the latter were increasingly perceived as a threat to traditional Judaism and Jewish causes.[24] Judaism, like Christianity, sought to attract adherents and sympathizers to expand their numbers and to gain material support. Sympathizers, known as "God-worshipers" (*theosebeis*), were attracted to Jewish monotheism and could be counted on as donors and supporters for Jewish building projects.[25] With the advent and spread of Christianity

---

21. Wayne A. Meeks. *The First Urban Christians* (New Haven: Yale University Press, 1983), 11;15.

22. Greg Woolf. *Rome: An Empire's Story* (Oxford: Oxford University Press, 2012), 260.

23. Meeks, *First Urban Christians,* 17.

24. Harnack, *Mission and Expansion of Christianity,* 56-59.

25. John Dominic Crosson and Jonathan L. Reed. *In Search of Paul* (New York: HarperSanFrancisco, 2004), 23-24.

and its evangelical mission, Judaism suddenly faced unexpected competition, where Christian missionaries like Paul and Barnabas sought not only to deprive Judaism of its Jewish base but also those who might otherwise become God Worshipers.

In addition to conflict with Jews, Christians were also the subject of controversy with regard to the Roman public and the Roman state as well. In the earliest days of the Christian mission, a developed antipathy arose toward the newly minted religion, which was poorly understood and the subject of significant misrepresentation. The Romans doubted the patriotism of the Christians because they refused to participate in the state cult, whose gods, they believed, had blessed the Roman state and ultimately granted it victory over its neighbors. The Christians' refusal to purchase or consume animals sacrificed to the Roman gods severely depressed livestock prices in some areas since the demand for both sacrificial victims and their meat were found wanting.[26] Of most concern to the Roman public was the nature of their Christian religious observance which, like the mysteries involved in the worship of the goddess Cybele, the rites of Bacchus, and other mystery religions, involved rituals that could only be known by those who were novices or catechumen or full members of the particular cult. Due to this secrecy, rumors circulating about the Christians were often as fantastic as the imagination of those who spread the rumors, with tales of Christians regularly engaging in incestuous rites, infanticide and human cannibalism among the more damning of those that were told.[27] These rumors inevitably fueled antipathy with the Roman public and led ultimately to a political climate favorable toward not only the delegitimization of Christianity as a competitor with traditional Roman cult but also outright persecution of the religion.

26. Pliny the Younger, governor of Bithynia, in a letter to the Emperor Trajan noted the decline of the market for beef resulting from the influence of Christians. The markets started once again to gain momentum after Christians were brought to trial in areas under his jurisdiction. See Pliny the Younger, *Epistles* 10.96.

27. See generally Stephen Benko, *Pagan Rome and the Early Christians* (Bloomington: Indiana University Press, 1986).

Finally, a significant source of conflict involving Christians within the Roman Empire arose as a result of rivalry between various sects within Christianity itself. While Christianity is often viewed as a unified religion, this perspective is more accurate to describe later Christianity than that which existed in the second and third centuries of the Common Era where theological doctrines, particularly those involving Christology, were insufficiently developed or not developed at all. As a result, a number of different perspectives could be found within early Christianity on issues such as the humanity and divinity of Jesus of Nazareth, the nature of evil, the efficacy of baptism, and many other issues. The resultant discord often manifest itself in more than simple bickering but, as the Donatist controversy demonstrated in North Africa, a dispute on doctrinal matters could even lead to murder.

It was in this milieu that Christianity found itself during the late second and third centuries of the Common Era when, as shall be discussed at a later point in this work, the Alexamenos Graffito is arguably to have been produced. This time period begins when anti-Christian rhetoric was ramping up, where Christians were more numerous than in prior centuries, and where Christian apologetics were beginning to face increased rhetorical opposition from traditional cult practitioners as they realized that Christianity posed an existential threat to traditional ritualistic and sacrificial methods and traditional objects of worship. Indeed, the concern of these individuals had about Christianity was not misplaced. The ancient world had not seen anything like this new philosophy which preached not just the equality of all human beings as the Stoic philosophers maintained but had gone beyond this to urge the essential brotherhood of all, threatening to tear down traditional walls of separation which had long enforced a dichotomy between master and slave, Patrician and Plebian, Roman and Barbarian.[28] So too, Christian doctrine imported a new accountability where every individual was called upon to make a profession of personal faith, where the supreme

28. Elmer Truesdell Merrill, "The Attitude of Ancient Rome Toward Religion and Religious Cults," *The Classical Journal* 15. 4 (January 1920), 201.

god was a singular and mysterious Holy Trinity, and where this same Holy Trinity was a jealous God and could tolerate the worship of no other.[29] Again, while monotheism was nothing new and had appeared recurrently in multiple civilizations up to and including that of the Romans, and while certain oriental mystery religions like Mithraism, the Magna Mater, and the Cult of Isis had elements of a doctrine of salvation, none dared to claim the title of being the singular truth and sole path to salvation nor had any attempted to thwart the worship of other gods. As late antiquities scholar Peter Brown has stated, "[t]he rise of Christianity altered profoundly the texture of the late Roman world. Yet in moral matters, the Christian leaders made almost no innovations. What they did was more crucial. They created a new group, whose exceptional emphasis on solidarity in the face of its own inner tensions ensured that its members would practice what pagan and Jewish moralists had already begun to preach."[30]

---

29. Trinitarian thought was ill defined in the late Second and Early Third Centuries and found its maturity largely in the fourth century which among other things codified the Trinity as an article of faith in the Nicene Creed. See generally Henry Chadwick. *The Early Church* (London: Penguin, 1990).

30. Peter Brown, "Late Antiquity" in *A History of Private Life.* ed. Paul Veyne. Translated by Arthur Goldhammer. (Cambridge: Belknap/Harvard University Press, 1987), 260.

CHAPTER THREE

Roman Polytheism

A People Who Worshiped All the Gods in the World

WITHIN THE CITY OF Rome cult practices were diverse. They encompassed not only the ritual practice of the family hearth and home, but also the State cultic ritual, which included the worship and veneration of a vast array of deities, not the least of which were the Capitoline Triad of Jupiter, Juno and Minerva, among many others. In terms of scope, it could be credibly stated, as did the Christian apologist Minucius Felix, that the Romans worshiped all the gods in the world.[1]

---

1. Minucius Felix, *Octavius* 6.2-3.

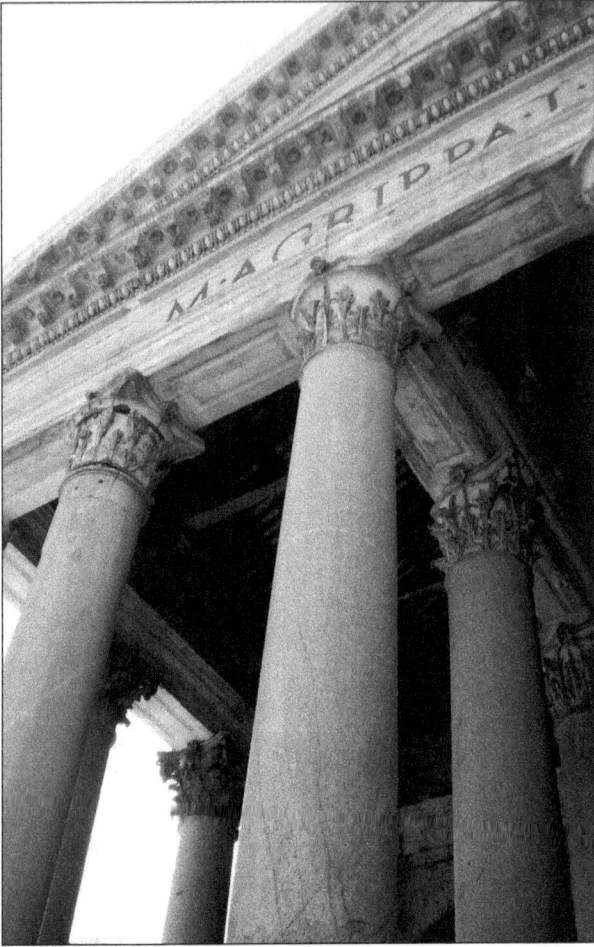

**The Roman Pantheon in Rome constructed as
a sanctuary for all of the Roman deities.**
Rome /Photo by Author

This was true for several reasons. First, the Romans saw a direct relation between their worship and veneration of the gods and the conferral of blessings and peace upon the Roman state (*pax deorum*).[2] It stood to reason, therefore, that the more gods

2. David S. Potter, "Roman Religion: Ideas and Action" in *Life, Death, and*

that were worshiped, the greater the chance that the Roman State would prosper.[3]

Capitolium of Jupiter, Juno, & Minerva
Dougga (Thugga), Tunisia/Photo by Author

Secondly, Roman religious cult was inherently a pragmatic scheme which was designed to systematically respond to prodigies, or perceived messages from the gods of their displeasure expressed as natural catastrophes, through religious innovations designed to appropriately respond to the crisis which encouraged innovation and worship and on occasion, an expansion of those gods which were worshiped.[4] This pragmatism was also reflected to a lesser extent in private cult practices where the gods chosen

---

Entertainment in the Roman Empire, ed. D.S. Potter and D.J. Mattingly (Ann Arbor: University of Michigan Press, 1999), 119-125.

3. Potter, "Roman Religion: Ideas and Action," 115.

4. Rupke, *Religion of the Romans,* 228-229.

for household worship would reflect the social and financial needs or emergencies of the household.[5]

So important was the relationship between the Romans and their gods that every effort was made to assure that this relationship continued and prospered. This meant that Roman public cult was entirely within the care of the Roman State controlled by permanent boards composed of high ranking citizens.[6] Furthermore, public religion in Rome was the monopoly of the Patricians who carefully controlled not only the manner in which the gods were worshiped but also which gods were worshiped.[7] Critical to the success of this relationship was proper observance of ritual (*sacra*); prediction (*auspicia*); and interpretation.[8]

Temple of Caelestis, (*Thugga (Douga), Tunisia*)

5. Rupke, *Religion of the Romans,* 81; Bodel, "Cicero's Minerva, Penates, and the Mother of the Lares," 251.

6. Rupke, *Religion of the Romans Religion of the Romans* 31-35.

7. Rupke, *Religion of the Romans,* 31-35.

8. Rupke, *Religion of the Romans,* 228-231; Potter, "Roman Religion: Ideas and Action," 134-159.

Sacra was established through the participation in established cult by the Roman people which could consist of a number of particular acts including ritual dances, processions, sacrifice, feasting and communal meals, prayer, and supplication, among other acts.[9] Integral to traditional Roman cult was the practice of divination which was divided into several groups of specialists. Augers sought to make predictions (*auspicia*) of the god's intent for the future by studying natural phenomena or the action of birds.[10] Other forms of interpretation of the future came from the insights provided by haruspices, whose ability to engage in divination arose from the careful inspection the entrails of sacred animals in accordance with established principles.[11]

Sometimes the gods were more direct in indicating what the future might hold for the Roman State. When religious ritual was lacking or where there was a spiritual misstep, the gods often warned the Romans of the fact to enable them to avoid the often dire consequences of transgression. One of the most notable was the appearance of prodigies, or events which were extraordinary in nature and believed by Roman authorities to have been sent by the gods as a warning that the *pax deorum* had been compromised.[12] Prodigies could include such diverse occurrences as lightning striking a state temple, the onset of plagues, or the broadcast of strange, often prophetic voices, seemingly coming from nowhere.[13] Once a prodigy had been identified and confirmed by the Senate, an innovation in cult practice was prescribed to expiate the prodigy, very often involving an alteration in worship to appease the offended god or the worship of differing divine entities.[14] Such alterations in worship could include gifts and sacrifices of precious metals to the

9. Rupke, *Religion of the Romans*, 22-23.

10. R. M. Ogilvie. *The Romans and Their Gods in the Age of Augustus* (New York: Norton, 1969) 56.

11. Ogilvie, *Romans and Their Gods in the Age of Augustus*, 65.

12. Ogilvie, *Romans and Their Gods in the Age of Augustus*, 58-59; Cicero, *De divinatione* 2.22.

13. Cicero, *De divinatione*, 2.22-32.

14. Ogilvie, *Romans and Their Gods in the Age of Augustus*, 62-63.

gods or the creation of festivals which the people were to observe.[15] On the rarest of occasions, even human sacrifices or victims were involved.[16] Where the Romans sought to alter their destiny by worship of different gods, they would not shrink from adopting the gods of their neighbors and enemies. In the course of their many wars with neighboring tribes and later nations, the Romans would often appropriate their enemy's gods, sometimes by outright theft of the gods from their shrines and temples (*evocatio*).[17]

The expansion of the number of gods worshiped by the Romans was not strictly the product of theft or enticement. A more than sizable number of gods of foreign extraction were peaceably adopted into Roman worship, particularly in the late Republican period and early empire, which were altogether foreign to the Italian peninsula. The cults of the Cybele, Isis, Zeus-Serapis, Magna Mater, Jupiter Heliopolitanus, Mithras, and Dionysus all originated from the East.[18] Despite general prejudices against non-native cults, a number of foreign cults were adopted with the blessing of the Roman Senate, including that of the Greek Asceleius, the Semitic Aphrodite of Mount Eryx, and the Phrygian Great Mother.[19] The cult of Cybele was officially recognized in 204 BCE following an agreement with the king of Pergamum.[20] Other cults came into circulation by various other means, such as through the commercial activies of Syrian merchants in search of profits scattered throughout Italy, Gaul, Spain, Africa, and in the Danubian countries, forming colonies and spreading their various religious cults. Non-citizen residents of urban centers, retaining their native culture, "establish[ed] local cults of their native gods."[21] Likewise,

---

15. Jorge at 229; Livy, *Ad Urba Condita* 22.1.8

16. See generally, Celia E. Schultz, "The Romans and Ritual Murder," *Journal of the American Academy of Religion* 78. 2 (June 2010): 516-541.

17. Livy, *Ad Urba Condita*, 5.21 1-7.

18. See generally Robert Turcan. *The Cults of the Roman Empire*. trans. Antonia Nevill (Oxford: Blackwell, 1992).

19. Turcan, *Cults of the Roman Empire*, 12.

20. Turcan, *Cults of the Roman Empire*, 13.

21. Francis Cumont, *Oriental Religions in Roman Paganism*. Translated by

soldiers stationed in far cast outposts like Brittania or Parthia took local women, raised families, and adopted the local gods and brought their worship back to the Italian peninsular when their tour of duty was over.[22]

Not every introduction of a foreign god into cultic practices was successful. In particular, the cultic worship of Bacchus (*Dionysis*), was disfavored due to its perceived negative effect on female morality. In addition, the cult's ritual practices so alarmed the Roman Senate that worship of Bacchus was effectively banned.[23] The Cult of Isis and Serapis also suffered similar disfavor, having statutes, altars, and private chapels destroyed by the Senate in the last century of the BCE as well as having its rituals prohibited as late as the reign of Tiberius. The cult of Isis later found acceptance and was formally deemed a licit religion by the time of Caligula, who erected the great temple of Isis Campensis on the Campus Martius in Rome.[24]

Grant Showerman (New York: Dover, 1956), 3-24.

22. Lawrence Keppie, *The Making of the Roman Army* (New York: Barnes and Noble 1984),147-148. For example, evidence of the worship of the Syrian god Ceres or Cybele and Mithras has been found on memorials and in the architectural remains of structures in and along Hadrian's wall. See generally Ronald Empleton and Frank Graham. *Hadrian's Wall* (New York: Dorset Press 1984).

23. Livy, *Ad Urbe Condita*, 39.16. 6-9.

24. Turcan, *Cults of the Roman Empire*, 90-91; Cumont, *Oriental Religions in Roman Paganism*, 83-84.

Penates

(Pompeii, Italy)

Whether such disapproval was in fact the product of moral concerns has been the subject of debate. At least one scholar attributes State restriction on such foreign cults with their popularity among urban plebeian, often of foreign extraction, and the corrosive effect upon "state solidarity" where such aliens were allowed to worship foreign, not native gods.[25]

On the level of the individual household, such religious pluralism was also evident in the private cult worship undertaken by the male head of the household and his family (*paterfamilias*). It has been said that the public cult "derived its nature and existence from the family, and not the family from the State."[26] The validity

25. Robert Birchman, *Porphyry: Against the Christians* (Boston: Brill, 2005), 18.

26. See generally Elmer Truesdell Merrill, "The Attitude of Ancient Rome Toward Religion and Religious Cults," *The Classical Journal* Vol. 15. No. 4

in such a statement resides mainly in the pluralism that was such an integral part of domestic cult. Families worshiped and venerated the protecting spirits of the *Lares*, their particular ancestral gods known as the *Penates*, as well as any number of other gods chosen by the head of the household, even those of the State pantheon.[27] Thus, it can reasonably be said that the public and private Roman cult promoted a general atmosphere of tolerance of a wide variety of religious expressions. However, this tolerance was by no means without limit and tolerance extended at one period could be entirely lacking in another. Some cult practices, even of a relatively domestic origin, would not be extended tolerance, whether due to their negative impact on Roman society at large, or out of concern that these practices eroded the solidarity of the Roman people in worshiping the gods that had made Rome such a success.

Finally, it should be said that non-native foreign religions were often viewed with suspicion by traditional minded Romans. This suspicion often progressed to ridicule and derision in private and, in a few circumstances, the public furor reached such a pitch that the Roman State intervened, banning the disfavored religious practices and initiating a program of public persecution. As it will be seen, while Christianity suffered mightily at the hands of Roman authorities, so too did other disfavored or illicit religious practices and the methods used to suppress religious expression were not reserved for Christianity alone.

(January 1920): 196–215.

27. Merrill, "Attitude of Ancient Rome," 198-199.

CHAPTER FOUR

Roman Intolerance Toward Non-Native Cults and Religions

OUR KNOWLEDGE OF ROMAN beliefs and attitudes toward Christianity and other religions that entered into the fabric of the Roman Republic and Empire is in large part informed by the extant literature of the first through the fourth centuries. Regrettably, the sources that survive are few and the perspectives expressed are hardly those of the average Roman in the empire. Rather, the primary sources that still serve as a reference for Roman opinion are largely confined to male Patrician Senatorial and Equestrian Class voices, rather than those of the Plebian "man on the street" or those of women or slaves. As will be seen, the Alexamenos Graffito, the main subject of this work, constitutes a rare occasion where the author was likely to be found as belonging to the lowest of Roman social classes.

An example of a voice that survives from antiquity is that of the Roman historian Gaius Suetonius Tranquillus, commonly known as Suetonius. Suetonius was from a modest North African family but rose to enjoy powerful connections with Pliny the Younger, who was both senator and later Governor of the Roman Province of Bithynia, not to mention the Emperors Trajan and Hadrian.[1] In his

1. James Uden "The Margins of Satire: Suetonius, Satura, and Scholarly

biography of the Emperor Nero, Suetonius had occasion to reference the new phenomena of Christianity, referencing Christians as men given to a new and mischievous superstition.[2] Suetonius' associate, Pliny the Younger, who was also an intimate of the Emperor Trajan, also had views on Christians that have survived. In one of his letters to his friend the Emperor Trajan, Pliny very well describes the antipathy of the Roman State toward the Christians in the second century in several of his letters. These letters all solicit from Trajan the proper procedure for prosecuting recalcitrant Christians. In the exchange between the Governor and the Emperor, Pliny describes Christian religious practice as being an "extravagant superstition" and "insanity" which is evidenced by the behavior of the Christians who are said to ignorantly persist, even under torture, to admit their affiliation with Jesus, something Pliny identified with "obstinacy and unbending perversity."[3]

In the same vein, the Greek philosopher Celsus, who wrote about the same time, also denigrated Christianity as a religion which merely recycled well-worn Greek ideas and portrayed Jesus as a second rate magician pulling off third-rate stunts and whose lack of divinity should be evident to anyone who considered the subject.[4] As for Christians themselves, Celsus portrayed them as nothing more than ". . .wool-workers, cobblers, laundry workers, and the most illiterate and bucolic yokels."[5]

Outside the polemic found in literature, there is also an oral tradition which likewise heaped abuse upon the Christians. While it is certainly hard to encapsulate what essentially amounts to rumor and hearsay, we are fortunate to have the writings of a third century Christian apologist, Municius Felix, who recorded

---

Outsiders in Ancient Rome," *American Journal of Philology* 141, 4 (Winter 2020), 575-601.

2. Suetonius, *Vita Neronis 4.16.*

3. Pliny the Younger, *Epistle.* 10.8

4. Origen, *Contra Celsum*. Trans. Henry Chadwick. (Cambridge: Cambridge University Press, 1953), 165.

5. See generally Celsus, *On the True Doctrine*. Trans. Joseph Hoffman (Oxford: Oxford University Press, 1987).

popular sentiment at the time.[6] Municius Felix well illustrated traditional Roman hostility toward the Christians through the words of Caecilius, the antagonist in his work, *Octavius*, who relates the common sentiment of the Roman streets concerning Christians and Christianity. Caecilius claims that Christians have corrupted the morals of society through their predilection for vice, as demonstrated by their incestuous relations with one another and their almost complete possession by illicit lust.[7] This immorality was openly on display at their regular banquets, where the Christian's would gather with all their children, sisters, and mothers, engage in incestuous relations with those assembled, and even practice murder and cannibalism.[8] With regard to the charges of murder and cannibalism, Caecilius informs his audience that Christian initiates at banquets are presented a dough-encrusted infant which, being bludgeoned, is consumed by the initiates, the blood lapped up and the limbs of the infant torn from the torso of the body and consumed.[9]

In addition to being labeled cannibals, incest practitioners, and murderers, the Christians were also proclaimed to be atheistic and unpatriotic. Unwilling to worship the gods, to participate in festivals and processions which showed the gods veneration, they undermined the state whose further success was conditioned upon the continued devotion of those within the Roman State. This was certainly the attitude of Pliny who viewed Christians to be addicted to a degenerate and extravagant cult whose practices and were seen to be the root cause of certain provincial economic difficulties.[10] Obeying their creed, Christians refrained from eating meat that had previously been sacrificed to the gods in the Roman

---

6. The report of Muncius Felix, who was a Christian, of rumours and slander against the Christians was also corroborated by Marcus Cornelius Fronto, who relates nearly the same story told by Felix, as Fronto came to hear the story from an unnamed citizen in Asia.

7. Minucius Felix, *Octavius*, 8-9.

8. Minucius Felix, *Octavius*, 8.4-5

9. Minucius Felix, *Octavius*, 9-5.6

10. Pliny the Younger, *Epistles*, 10.8.

temples. Having persuaded their fellow countrymen of validity of their beliefs, temples in Bithynia were ". . . almost entirely deserted . . . and the sacred rites had been allowed to lapse."[11] As a result, the meat of the temple sacrifices had ceased to be sold thereby depriving the temples of critical revenue.[12] Depriving the gods of their temples, their sacrifices, and of their priests with a means of livelihood in an orthopraxic society where everything depended upon the *quid pro quo* between the gods could only spell catastrophe for the Roman State as far as Pliny could see it.

These views, taken together, provide an approximation of the commonly held views of the Romans toward the Christians who were increasingly appearing in their midst.[13] As problematic and extreme as these attacks against Christianity might have been, they were not without precedent. The second century polemics employed against the Bacchanalian cultic rites were similarly coarse and likewise involved similar invective. While obscure, Bacchic rites originated with Greek worship of the god, Dionysis, with whom the Romans identified with their god, Bacchus. At least one early cultic group was associated with a burial society whose cemetery was restricted to burial to only those who had been initiated into the Bacchic rites.[14] The cult, from a fairly early simplicity, developed into a complex organization with a number of specialized offices and positions within the hierarchy, including "god bearers"; "holy herdsmen"; "bearers of the winnowing fan"; "guardians of the sacred cave"; "holy bacchants"; "bacchant initiates"; and "novices", among others. Its rites were a mystery but included its dogma included a least a suggestion that Bacchic initiates could enjoy the hope of eternal life.[15]

---

11. Pliny the Younger, *Epistles,* 10.8.

12. Pliny the Younger, *Epistles,* 10.8.

13. Benko, Stephen, *Pagan Rome and the Early Christians* (Bloomington: Midland, 1986), 54-55.

14. "The Great Bacchic Inscription at Tusculum" in *Ancient Roman Religion.* ed.: Frederick C. Grant (New York: The Liberal Arts Press, 1957), 56.

15. Grant, "Great Bacchic Inscription at Tusculum," 56.

The historian Livy is our primary source for evidence for Roman acts of repression against the cult. According to Livy, the Roman consuls had gathered an assembly of citizens in Rome to address them about the impending danger of the Bacchanalia which was starting to take root in the city. Livy wrote that these same consuls were alarmed that the Bacchanalia, long celebrated all over Italy, was now within the City in many places. Moreover, their ever present cries at night was believed by some to be a form of worship of the gods, by others as merely a pastime.[16] Regardless, alarm was taken because of the matriarchal nature of Baccanalian devotion as well as the excesses which devotees engaged which included debauched behavior and excessive use of wine.[17]

Temple of Isis
Pompeill /Photo by Author

As was stated at the time, while the cultic conspiracy had not strength in the beginning, the increased popularity of the

16. Livy, *Ad Urba Condita* 39.15.
17. Livy, *Ad Urba Condita* 39.15.

cult among women made the likelihood of a clash with Roman authorities increasingly likely by the day.[18] Livy had even more to say with even greater vitriol to cast upon the Baccanalia and its practitioners, attributing to the cult perjury, poisonings, secret murders, and the promiscuity. Predictably, public sentiment against the Bacchanalian rites materialized into legislation prohibiting the cult's practice and leading to the arrest of the cult's priesthood and execution of a number of the members of the cult.[19] Though perhaps more as a political reaction at the time of the first Triumvirate than an expression of public hostility, the shrines of Isis were ordered demolished. These same shrines were later restored, only to be destroyed again, the casualties of a raging civil war, until the worship of Isis became finally established during the reign of Octavian Caesar.[20]

As can be seen, something as basic as private criticism of a particular cultic practice could very easily turn into public hostility and even small scale physical violence and disruption. However, when this hostility became the impetus for Senatorial or Imperial action against a particular religion or cultic practice, there could be significant and widespread consequences. The Roman State persecution of the Christians is an apt example.

The first recorded public persecution of Christians began during the first century during the reign of Nero (54-68 CE). Nero's persecution saw the initiation of organized, state sponsored oppression based not so much as any particular wrong committed but upon the mere confession of being a follower of Christ.[21] Once identified as such, Christians were reportedly executed in the most brutal of fashions, the victims being ". . .covered with the skins of beasts, [and] were torn by dogs and perished, or were nailed to crosses, or were doomed to the flames."[22]

18. Livy, *Ad Urba Condita* 39.8-9.

19. Livy, *Ad Urba Condita* 39.14.3-14.10.

20. Valerie M. Warrior. *Roman Religion: A Sourcebook* (Newburyport, MA: Focus Publishing, 2001), 107.

21. Tacitus, *Annales* 15.44.

22. Tacitus, *Annales* 15.44.

Over the ensuing centuries, such forms of persecution continued, albeit in differing and somewhat moderated forms. Among the more notorious who persecuted the Christians, under Domitian (81-96 CE), Christians continued to be oppressed as atheists and the punishment dispensed was execution and deprivation of property. In the reign of Valerian (253-260 CE.) persecution took a more sadistic turn. Eusebius, quoting a letter of Dionysis, the Bishop of Rome, portrays a renewal of persecution shortly after Valerian's rise to power. Eusebius accuses Valerian, rightly or wrongly, of all manner of crimes, from cutting the throats of unfortunate boys and tearing out the vital parts of babies to using children as sacrificial victims.[23] How much of Eusebius' description was factual is debatable, especially in light of the fact that a premium was placed upon martyrdom in the early church as a vehicle for increasing the numbers of the faithful. Christian persecution, whether it consisted of torture or the ultimate penalty of crucifixion, was a form of rhetoric, with every action taking on symbolic significance. For the Christian, persecution was mostly a test of commitment and faith in Christian doctrine but had wider dimensions. The persecution by Roman authorities and the creation of martyrs for the faith validated the prophetic words of Jesus of Nazareth that the end times were coming to pass. where the individual believer would be delivered up to be afflicted, even unto death for their faith[24] This validation of the truth of Jesus' prophecy was a powerful tool for recruitment of others to the Christian ranks who might have otherwise not been persuaded. For the Roman State, however, persecution served the goal of ultimately denigrating, discrediting, and in the end, eradicating Christianity which was considered an existential threat to the Roman State. When all other rhetorical strategies failed, the final word was crucifixion which was not simply killing but was also a carefully crafted message which others would do well to receive: that if you threatened the Roman State, you could be assured that you would suffer an unclean, shameful, unmanly, and unworthy death.

23. Eusebius Pamphilius. "Church History" in *Nicene and Post Nicene Fathers*. Ed. Philip Schaff. (Grand Rapids, MI: Erdmans, 1890), V. I-VII

24. Matthew 24:9

CHAPTER FIVE

The Geography of the Alexamenos Graffito

Rome, the Palatine Hill, the Domus Augustana, and the Pedagogium

A Brief History of the City Of Rome

THE ORIGINS OF ROME are clouded by the lack of a concrete and surviving archaeological record and many of the claims made about the city are based on the interpretation of very scant evidence. However, there is a modest amount of agreement about a few facts by scholars. One of them is that the site on which Rome is situated has been continuously occupied since the Bronze Age.[1] Rome's initial urban core was probably humble in nature, consisting of a number of iron age huts on at least a few of Rome's hills, in particular the Palatine and Esquilline, where such huts have been excavated, but probably also on the Quirinal, Aventine, and Caelian hills as well.[2] The village that was to become

---

1. Woolf, "Beyond Romans and Natives," 32.

2. Amanda Claridge. *Oxford Archeological Guides. Rome* (Oxford: Oxford University Press, 1998), 4.

the City of Rome was situated on the banks of the Tiber River the location of which was no doubt informed by mundane practical considerations. However, tradition also makes the claim that the location of the village was also the product of religious inquiry, where the site was particularly chosen after consultation with the gods through augury.[3]

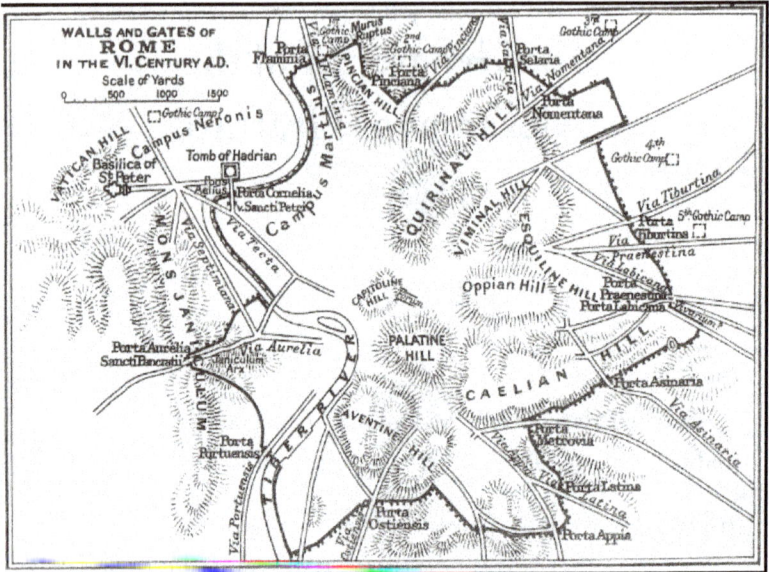

Walls and Seven Hills of Rome
Public Domain

Regardless of the motivations behind the choice in location, the city's early founders, probably a number of clans and families of various status, began the process of urbanization of the raw landscape, their building inspired by cultural influences from Greece and Phoenicia, as well as that which came from the surrounding tribal communities.[4]

3. Fustel de Coulanges, *The Ancient City* (Garden City, NY: Doubleday Anchor, 1864), 136.

4. Woolf, "Beyond Romans and Natives," 34.

At some point around 750 to 700 BCE, the settlement began to develop economically, with certain segments of the population taking on economic specialization such as the cultivation of olives, viticulture, and the production of pottery.[5] Increased wealth, in part the result of developing industry and resultant trade, led to the creation of a more substantial material culture. By 650 BCE, large stone houses began to be built where previously there had only been only those made of mud and daub.[6] Additionally, by 625 BCE, public spaces and public buildings were erected around a central forum.[7] It was during this period, extending to possibly 600 BCE to 535 BCE, that a fortified wall was also built, first of raised earthen walls (*agger*) and ditches (*fossa*), then of stone and earth following a consecrated path (*pomerium*) that enclosed the Palatine, Quirinal, Viminal, and part of the Equiline communities.[8] Pliny the Elder estimated that the circumference of the walls which surrounded Rome and the Seven Hills was approximating thirteen miles with the city being divided into fourteen districts.[9] He also noted that originally there were only three gates to the city, but that by his time in the first century of the Common Era, that number had grown to thirty seven gates.[10]

The construction of public buildings also included the erection of temples to the public gods. In 509 BCE, the summit of the Capitoline Hill was crowned with a newly built, three cella Temple of Jupiter, Juno, and Minerva, a project that followed the previous establishment of a Capitolium to the same three gods on the Quirinal Hill and a Temple to Diana on the Aventine Hill.[11]

5. Christopher S. Mackay, *Ancient Rome* (Cambridge: Cambridge University Press, 2004), 10.

6. Mackay, *Ancient Rome,* 12.

7. Mackay, *Ancient Rome,* 12.

8. Arthur E.R. Boak, *A History of Rome* (New York: MacMillan, 1955), 38.

9. J.B. Ward-Perkins, *Cities of Ancient Greece and Italy: Planning in Classical Antiquity* (New York: George Braziller, 1974), 40.

10. Pliny, *Natural History* 3.9.

11. Axel Boerthius, *Etruscan and Early Roman Architecture* (London: Penguin, 1987), 110-112. Cella are half-barrell shaped indentations in a wall which provide for the display of statuary.

Later temples of other deities were constructed in the ensuing century including the Temple of Saturn and Castor and Pollux on the Forum Romana and that of Mercury, Ceres, Liber, and Libera on the Aventine Hill.[12]

While the development of the City of Rome may, up to this point, seem to be somewhat in accordance with a grand evolutionary plan, the reality was quite to the contrary. Unlike many of the other cities and towns that developed in the Republican period and the period of the early Empire, Rome, for the most part, "grew without ever achieving a rational plan."[13] Exceptions to this haphazard development scheme did exist. For example, the Emperor Augustus gave the city a logical structure, dividing it into 14 regions (*regiones*) with additional subdivision into an expandable number of quarters (*vici*).[14] Likewise, Marcus Agrippa's development of the Campus Martius and erection of the Pantheon under the Emperor Trajan followed along lines contemplated by the Emperor Augustus to restore Roman religious shrines and temples and to reinvigorate piety through its public structures.[15] In addition, various other structures in the city's *Forum Romana* were also rehabilitated, public sculptures added, and honorary arches were inserted at strategic points throughout the city to serve as "excellent billboards for propaganda and useful urban markers, permanently associating particular events or achievements with specific sites" and "demarcat[ing] distinct spaces".[16]

---

12. Boerthius, *Etruscan and Early Roman Architecture*, 112

13. Ward-Perkins, *Cities of Ancient Greece and Italy*, 40.

14. Andrew Wallace-Hadrill, *Mutatas Formas: The Augustan Transformation of Roman Knowledge in The Cambridge Companion to the Age of Augustus* (Cambridge: Cambridge University Press, 2005), 77.

15. Diane Favro, "Making Rome a World City" in *The Cambridge Companion to the Age of Augustus*. ed. Karl Galinsky (Cambridge: Cambridge University Press, 2005): 240-249.

16. Favro, "Making Rome a World City," 240-249.

The Palatine Hill

Rome's seven "hills" originally offered early inhabitants respite from the rages of a flooding Tiber River and other dangers of the Iron Age. Over time, each took on a unique character, imparted largely as a result of the functions each hill eventually took on. For example, the Capitoline Hill which is western most hill, became associated with the Roman State administration and the cults of the Roman State, The eastern Esquiline Hill became the site of the entertainments and recreation, most notably featuring the Colosseum, triumphal arches, and baths.

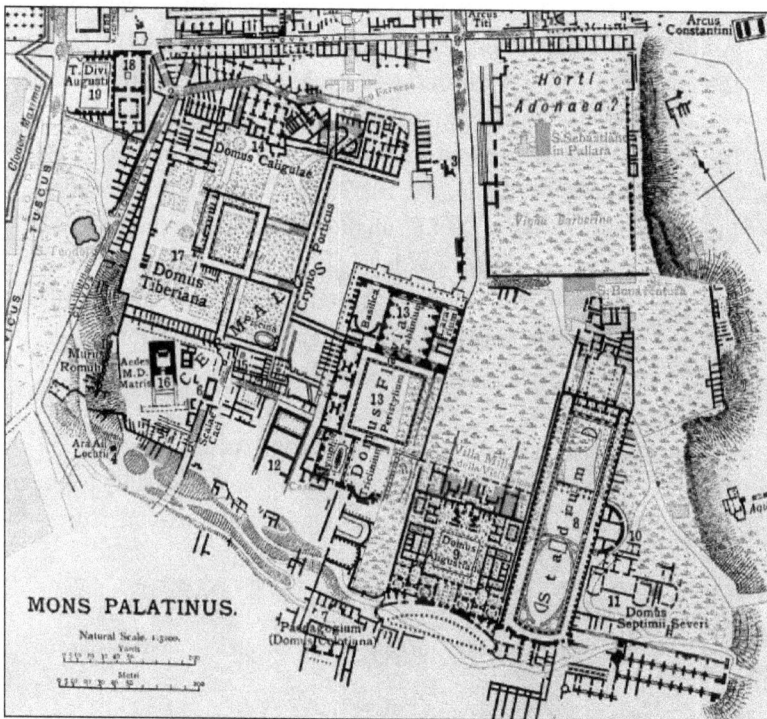

Map of Palatine Hill showing Domus Augustus and Pedagogium (lower center)

Public Domain

The central Palatine Hill lies to the east of the Tiber valley and has a summit which is only 164 feet above sea level.[17] The etymology of the name is uncertain but a number of ancient authors, including Dionysius of Haricarnassus, Livy, Pliny, and Solinus attribute the origin of the name from *Pallantion*, the Arcadian home of Evander, who is said to have founded the first settlement on the hill.[18] It is this same Evander who is said by Livy to have instituted the festival of the Lupercalia on the Palatine, an annual event in honor of the god, Pan.[19] Perhaps more than any other of the six hills of Rome, the Palatine was one of the most significant historically. It was reputed to be the original home of Romulus, the founder of the city, whose hut was located on the western slope. A number of cultic structures were also associated with the Palatine, including the Temple of the Magma Mater, an enormous, six columned, pro-style temple dedicated to the imported Phrygian goddess, Cybele, as well as the equally sizeable Temple of Victory, the Temple of Apollo, and the Temple of the Sun erected by the third century Emperor Elagabalus, dedicated to the god, Sol Evictus.[20] Most importantly, as it relates to the Alexamenos Graffito, the Palatine Hill was long regarded as a preferred residential area for Rome's elite, including a number of Imperial families, beginning with Octavian Caesar, later to be known as the Emperor Augustus.[21] Situated on the slopes of the hill are grand houses *(domus)*, palaces, and other structures constructed to house the imperial retinue of not only Augustus, but also Tiberius, Nero, Elagabalus, and Septimius Severus.[22] Outside of these, structures

17. Ministero per i Beni e le Attivita Culturali sopintendenza Archeologica de Roma. *The Palatine*. (Milan: Electa 1998), 3.

18. Ministero per i Beni e le Attivita Culturali sopintendenza Archeologica de Roma, *Palatine*, 3-4.

19. Livy, *Ad Urba Condita* 1.4.

20. Ministero per i Beni e le Attivita Culturali sopintendenza Archeologica de Roma, *Palatine*, 28.

21. Rudolfo Lanciani, *The Ruins and Excavations of the Paletione: A Companion Book for Students and Travelers*. Boston: Houghton Mifflin, 1897, 106–107.

22. Ministero per i Beni e le Attivita Culturali sopintendenza Archeologica

such as triumphal arches, baths, and aqueducts were erected by the Emperors Claudius, Titus, and Maxentius.[23]

Particularly significant for the focus of this work is the southernmost edge of the southern quadrant of the Palatine Hill upon which lies a complex of buildings of differing ages. These buildings are juxtaposed next to each other and include several imperial residential structures, including the palatial Domus Augustustana and the Pedegogium. Included within the Pedegogium is an additional structure, sometimes identified as the Domus Gelatiano. It is within this particular substructure that the Alexamenos Graffito was located. An understanding of the history and archeological contexts of all the structures surrounding and proximate to the Graffito will better help illuminate its origin and significance as a particularized commentary on Christianity.

The Domus Augustana/Flavia

The Domus Augustana or Domus Flavia, a large palace structure which dominates the lower south eastern quadrant of the Palatine Hill, was constructed in part by the Flavian Emperors Vespasian and Domitian in the latter part of the first century of the Common Era.[24] The structure housed a number of rooms from banquet facilities and gardens to a throne and reception room and an auditorium.[25] These structures were later supplemented by construction which occurred during the reigns of the Emperors Trajan and Hadrian.[26] It was during this period of expansion that the Domus Augustana was connected with the nearby Circus Maximus, a popular chariot racing venue, by a bridge and the creation of

de Roma, *Palatine,* 19.

23. Ministero per i Beni e le Attivita Culturali sopintendenza Archeologica de Roma, *Palatine,* 19.

24. Ulrike Wulf-Rheidt, "The Palaces of the Roman Emperors on Palatine in Rome" in *The Emperor's House.* ed Michael Featherstone, et. Al. (Berlin: Walter de Gruyter GmbH 2015), 6.

25. Wulf-Rheidt, "Palaces of the Roman Emperors," 10-11.

26. Wulf-Rheidt, Palaces of the Roman Emperors," 12-13.

an imperial box (*pulvinar*) for the use of the Imperial Family for viewing the chariot races.[27]

The Pedagogium

As an adjunct structure of the Domus Augustana, the Pedagogium was erected by the Emperor Domitian as a school for imperial slaves, notably individuals in the service of the Emperor who acted as pages.[28]

Pedagogium

Rodolfo Lanciani/Public Domain

27. Wulf-Rheidt, Palaces of the Roman Emperors," 13.

28. Ruldolfo Amedeo Lanciani. *The Ruins and Excavations of the Palatine: A Companion Book for Students and Travelers* (Boston: Houghton Mifflin, 1897), 185-186; Horace Marucchi. *The Roman Forum and the Palatine According to the Latest Discoveries* (Rome: Desclee Lefebvre, 1906), 320;

It is a rectangular building approximately 50 meters wide and approximately 15 meters in depth.[29] The structure has a number of rooms which are arrayed both in the interior as well as along the exterior walls. Most of the rooms are rectangular in shape and appear to be bedrooms (*cubiculum*). One notable exception is a semi-circular alcove which may have been a washroom or bathing area.[30] The Pedagogium was two stories and was composed of a three-part structure with a north-south orientation. The upper, northerly compound, after its original use as an imperial palace, is believed to have subsequently housed the page school.[31] A number of the scholars who have surveyed the site agree that the site had a multiplicity of purposes rather than one continuous function. For example, Peter Keegan notes that evidence exists not only for the Pedagogium to have served as a page school but also possibly as a prison for slaves, as a barracks for foreign soldiers, as a meeting place for administrative officials (*procurators*), and as an infirmary for the Circus Maximus, among other possible uses.[32]

The Domus Augustana and the Pedagogium were connected through the Domus' lower portions to the south which included a building with an atrium and the previously-mention platform/bridge built in proximity to the Circus Maximus. As mentioned before, there is some evidence that this bridge was constructed for the use of the emperor, who was an enthusiast for the Green chariot racing faction, to fraternize with the drivers who assembled just outside the palace door.[33] Other elements were

29. Fernidand Becker, *Das Spott-Crucifix der Römishen Kaiser paläste* (Breslau: Max Mälzer, 1866), 10.

30. Becker, *Spott-Crucifix der Römishen Kaiser paläste*, 10.

31. Lanciani, *Ruins and Excavations of the Palatine*, 185-186.

32. Peter Keegan. *Roman Slavery and Roman Material Culture*. Conference Paper, The Sixth E. T. Salmon Conference in Roman Studies: Roman Slavery and Roman Material Culture. McMaster University, Hamilton, Ontario. September 28-29, 2007, 5. The Caelian Hill was one of the seven hills of Rome and was proximate to the Palatine Hill where the domus Gelatiana is found.

33. Lanciani, *Ruins and Excavations of the Palatine*, 185-186; Van Deman at 102-103. . See also Suetonius, Caligula, 8.18, which references the Gelotian House as being near the Maeniana, a structure of houses with balconies

added to the Pedagogium by later emperors. For instance, John Henry Middleton in the nineteenth century described a colonnade *(porticus)* at the lower level of the structure consisting of a row of Corinthian columns which he dated to the time of Septimius Severus (193-211 CE).[34] Additionally, Peter Keegan more recently notes building components and residual paintings which have their origin in the reigns of not only Septimius Severus but also Domitian (81-96 CE), Trajan (98-117 CE), Hadrian (117-138 CE) and possibly Antonius Pius (138-161 CE).[35]

---

overlooking the Circus, which was also the emperor's roost when watching the games : *"Comisit et subitos, cum e Gelotiana apparatum Circi prospicientem pauci ex proximus Maenianis postulassent".*

34. John Henry Middleton. *Ancient Rome in 1888* (Edinburgh: Adam and Charles Black 1888), 124. H.W. Benario suggests also that the structure is of a Severan date but adds that ". . .the name is dubious since Caligula probably included the Domus Gelotiana within his palace." Benario, H.W. *Rome of the Severi.* Latomis. T. 17, Fasc. 4 (OCTOBRE-DÉCEMBRE 1958), 716.

35. Keegan, *Roman Slavery and Roman Material Culture,* 3-4.

—— PART TWO ——

THE ALEXAMENOS
GRAFFITTO EXAMINED

CHAPTER SIX

The Alexamenos Graffito

The Physical Description

THE SYSTEMATIC EXCAVATION OF the Palatine Hill which led to the discovery of the Alexamenos Graffito began in the first half of the eighteenth century. This work, initiated and funded by such personages as the Duke of Parma and the future Pope Pius XI, was interrupted for a considerable period of time until excavations resumed at some point between 1857 to 1862.

Domus Gelatiana
Rodolpho Lanciani/Public Domain

This renewed effort was championed by the Pontifical government in Rome and Emperor Napoleon III, whose empire extended at that time to include the city and large sections of the Italian Peninsula.[1] The work was conducted on two opposite sides of the Palatine Hill, on one side the area near the Circus Maximus was being brought to light, including the Domus Augustana and Pedagogium where the Alexamenos Graffito was located.[2] Other work was conducted in earnest on the summit of the Palatine. Of particular significance as it relates to the archaeological work undertaken near the Circus Maximus was the excavation of the Pedagogium and the Domus Gelatiana, which is southern adjunct of that building.

1. Horace Marucchi, *The Roman Forum and the Palatine* (Paris: Deselee Lefebvre, 1906), 286.

2. Marucchi, *Roman Forum and the Palatine*.

Wall within Domus Gelatina showing graffiti
Rodolpho Lanciani/ Public Domain

The Domus Gelatiana consists of a series of small vaulted rooms, once several stories high, with a Porticus or colonnade of Corinthian columns in front, at the lower level.[3] These rooms were partly clad in marble and in part covered with painted stucco.[4] On those areas where stucco was the exterior covering, a number of the graffiti were found on the plaster walls of a corridor running the width of the building from which access to a number of rooms and a bathing area can be obtained.[5] The Alexamenos Graffito was merely one of a number of graffiti found on the plaster walls in the structure.[6]

Among the inscriptions that can be found on the walls of this area are those of what were likely youths who attended the Pedagogium (i.e. "*Corinthus exit de Pedagogio*"; and "*Marianus afer exit*

3. John Henry Middleton, *Ancient Rome in 1888*. (Edinburgh: Adam and Charles Black, 1888), 124.

4. Middleton, *Ancient Rome in 1888,* 124.

5. Middleton, *The Remains of Ancient Rome*. Vol. 1. London: Adama and Charles Black (1892), 208.

6. Lanciani, *Ruins and Excavations of the Palatine*, 121.

de pedagogio").[7] At one point there was a graffito, now destroyed, of an ass working a grist mill with the caption "*Ego Laboravi Et Proderit Tibi* or "I have labored and you yourself have benefited."[8] An additional references has been made to an inscription reading "VDN" which has been interpreted to mean "*Verna domini nostril*" or "Verna our master".[9]

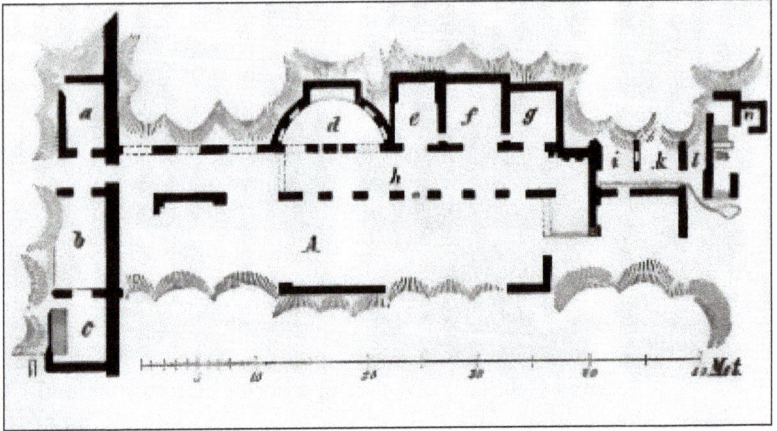

Floorplan of Domus Gelatiana
Ferdinand Becker/Public Domain

Aside from the graffiti found in the Domus pertaining to life in the Pedagogium, there have also been found graffiti which make apparent reference to Christianity. For example, one inscription references the cognomen "*Libanus*" with an additional inscription underneath reading "*Episcopus*" (overseer or bishop). This phrase is repeated in abbreviated fashion lower on the wall where an inscription reads "*Libanus Epi[scopus]*."[10] In addition, there is a Greek inscription, ΒΟΕΤΙΑ ΕΠΙΤΕΥ ΒΑΛΕΟΨ which Horace Marucci has translated to mean "Help comes from the god king". Whether

7. Lanciani, *Ruins and Excavations of the Palatine,* 121.

8. Lanciani, *Ruins and Excavations of the Palatine,* 121.

9. Becker at 12

10. Becker at 12.

this is a reference to Jesus of Nazareth or not might ordinarily be a matter of conjecture. However, the inscription's proximity to the Alexamenos Graffito, which is arguably a Christian reference, adds more probability that the Greek inscription is also a reference to Christianity.

Other claims related to the existence of Christian inscriptions on the walls which have not been adequately established or have been soundly disputed. For example, the Italian scholar Raphael Garrucci in 1857 went so far to claim the existence of multiple *Chi Rho* monograms on the same walls referenced above.

The Alexamenos Grafitto
Rodolpho Lanciani/ Public Domain

While there is presently no way to substantiate these claims, German scholar Ferdinand Becker, who had the opportunity to see the graffiti personally, disputes the claim as false with some discussion.[11] The most significant potential reference to an inscription related to Christianity is the Alexamenos Grafitto. As this inscription is the main subject matter of this work's inquiry, a more elaborate analysis is warranted which follows.

Analysis of the Alexamenos Graffito

The Alexamenos Graffito is so named because of the Graffito's principle subject matter is Alexamenos, whose god is portrayed as a crucified an ass-headed character. The Graffito itself measures .39 meters in height and .35 meters in width.[12] The field of the image is populated with two figures separated by a slight distance, a primary text, and a solitary textual figure, particularly a "Y" or an upsilon. The first figure, clearly hominid, is to the left of the field and appears to be gesturing toward the second figure bears the head of a horse or an ass. A Greek caption separates the two figures stating ΑΛΕΞΑΜΕΝΟΣ ΖΕΒΕΤΕ ΘΕΟΝ which translates as "Alexamenos worships his God."[13] Above both figures is what appears to be the Greek letter "Υ" (*upsilon*). who appears to be affixed to or resting astride a cross. The second figure, although also clearly hominid, bares the head of an ass and is situated to the right of the first figure.

The Hominid Figure

Shortly after the discovery of the Graffito, the Ferdinand Becker sought to interpret the presentation of the first hominid figure. His

11. Becker at 11-12.

12. Mary Beard, John North and Simon Price. *The Religions of Rome* V.2 (Cambridge: Cambridge University Press, 1998), 57.

13. Lanciani, *Ruins and Excavations of the Palatine,* 122. Beard, North, and Price translate this as "Alexamenos worships god". *Id.* At 58.

interpretation was two-fold, referencing both the dress and the gesture of the figure. As to the hominid figure's dress, he noted that the figure is clad not in a toga, the official garment of the Roman State, but in the less formal dress of a tunic.[14]

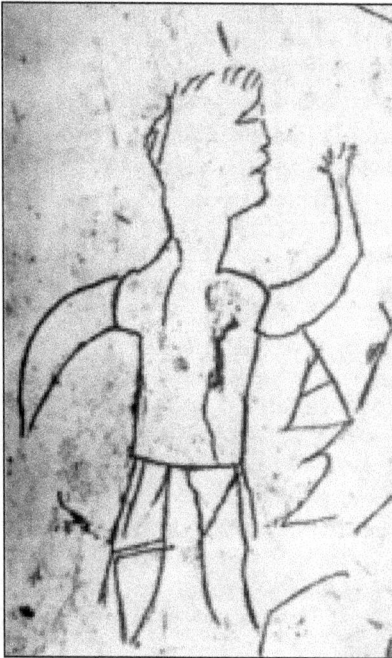

Hominid Figure
Rodolpho Lanciani/ Public Domain

The toga was the badge of Roman citizenship *par excellance.*[15] As fashion, the toga became more and more associated with formal dress, though it never reached the point of becoming archaic.[16] The tunic, on the other hand, was always associated with informality. While Becker merely points out this less formal state of dress and

14. Becker at 21. Becker uses the word "Hausekleid" or "house dress".

15. F.R. Cowell. *Life in Ancient Rome.* (New York: Capricorn Books, 1975), 72.

16. Cowell, *Life in Ancient Rome,* 72.

draws no overt implication from it, that does not mean that the fact is unimportant to the over-all meaning of the graffito. Rather to the contrary, the fact that a toga is not worn could imply that the figure wearing it is not a Roman citizen (i.e. barbarian) or that the worship he engages in is less than a serious affair. Either way, there are potential polemical implications in the choice of dress imposed upon the first hominid figure which will be important when one considers the other details Becker addresses.

With regard to these other details, Becker notes that the figure, positioned as he is with his hand proximate to his mouth and faced toward the second figure, is engaged in a ceremonial kiss.[17]

Exemplar of Roman Drapery of a god in the Toga Virilis
Thugga (Dougga), Tunisia/Photo by Author

The Latin *adorare* and the Greek προοκυνειν ("proskyne-sis") were both gestures of secular and sacred veneration which

---

17. Becker at 21.

involved the use of a kissing gesture.[18] *Adorare*, as it is particularly associated with hand kissing, directs the kiss toward the subject of veneration. Contemporary scholar, Berthe M. Marti, has traced the history of the gesture as a form of verbal linguistic and has found numerous references to the act of *adorare*, from the early empire in the works of Valerius Maximus and Tacitus to the more mature empire of Apuleus and Pliny. Of the textual references to adorare, Pliny the Elder in his *Natural History* describes the act as "*[i]n adorando dextram ad osculum referimus totumque corpus circumagimus*" ("In veneration, we kiss the right hand and we bring back around the whole body") as early as the first century, which would be congruent with the time period the *domus* was being used as a *paedagogia*.[19] The North African Roman author Apuleius, who wrote his *Metamorphosis* in the second century, makes a more explicit statement of the gesture, stating that "*[e]t admoventes oribus suis dexteram primore digito in erectum pollicem residente, ut ipsam Venerem prorsus deam religiosis adorationibus venerabantur.*"("And you move to the right side of the face the first finger in extension to the place of the thumb, as you pay direct homage to Venus through sacred worship").[20] It is interesting to note that in both Pliny and Apuleius, the act of adorare involves the right side of one's person. While the companion text of the Graffito particularly references worship by Alexamenos, it is highly likely that the act of worship being portrayed by the first figure, directed as it is toward the second figure, is an act of adorare. Nonetheless, as Becker, Hogg, and Keegan note, the figure uses the *left* arm to carry out the gesture of veneration.[21] This again a suggests polemical motive, portraying Alexamenos as a rube or hayseed, unaware of the proper method of venerating a god. When coupled with the first *foi pas* imposed on the hominid figure by the graffito's creator, some evidence begins to

18. Berthe M. Marti, "Proskynesis and Adorare" *Language.* 12 (Oct.-Dec. 1936): 273.

19. Pliny the Elder, *Naturalis Historia*, XXVIII: 27-28; Marti at 279-281.

20. Apuleius, *Metamorphoseon*, IV: 28; Marti at 279.

21. Becker at 22; Hogg at 35; Keegan, (2014), 108.

accumulate that the graffito is not a sincere representation of a Al-examenos' religious worship but rather an unflattering portrayal of the same. Contemporary scholars, most notably Peter Keegan, appear to generally concur with Becker's analysis.[22]

The Ass-Headed Hominid

The second figure in the field, that of the ass-headed hominid, is notable due to being the subject of religious veneration; due to being a bi-furcated, half-animal and half-human being; and because the second figure appears to be crucified. If the fore-going assumptions regarding that the first figure is engaged in an act adorare, then the question naturally arises as to the identity of the second figure such that it would warrant such veneration.

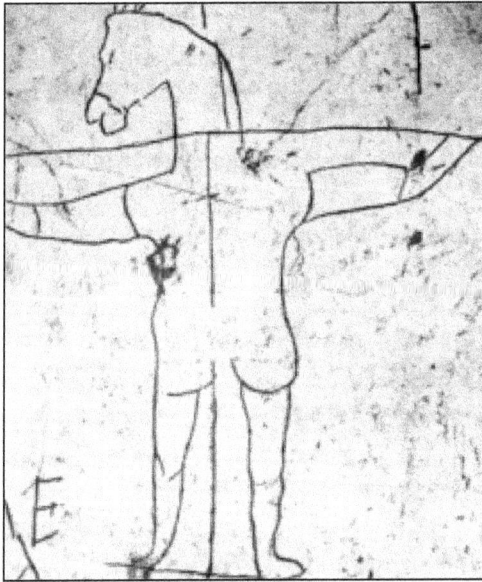

Ass-Headed Hominid
Rodolpho Lanciani/Public Domain

22. Keegan, *Grafitti in Antiquity*, 108.

The most commonly referenced interpretation of the identity of ass-headed hominid is that of Jesus of Nazareth represented in a polemical form. This view is adopted by Lanciani, Becker, and Hogg in the nineteenth century, and more recently in the scholarship by Mary Beard, John North, Simon Price and Peter Keegan.[23] On the other hand, John Henry Middleton, one of several nineteenth century commentators, rejected such an interpretation, instead indicating that the depiction was ". . .probably a scene of Gnostic worship, representing the Egyptian God Anubis."[24] Horace Marucci, an Italian contemporary of Lanciani and Becker and also writing in the nineteenth century, references the German philologist Moriz Haupt as positing a similar theory-that the ass-headed hominid was the Egyptian warrior god Set.[25] In the same vein, Richard Wünsch, focusing upon the "Y" or upsilon figure to the right of the ass's headed hominid, likewise deduces that the depiction is one of Gnostic worship of Typhon-Seth.[26] The basis of Wünsch's conjecture is based upon Roman curse-tablets where, according to Wünsch, the same "Y" symbol always stands at the right of a wild ass's head which acts as a portrayal of the deity Typhon-Seth.[27]

Becker argues that the depiction probably represents a polemic against Christianity rather than a sincere demonstration of veneration for Gnostic Egyptian deities, an argument he advances most compellingly through reference to Tertullian.[28] Indeed, the Christian apologist, Tertullian, who, in his *Apology*, does make reference to a new representation of the Christian god

23. Rudolfo Lanciani, *Ruins and Excavations of Ancient Rome*. (Boston: Houghton, Mifflin, 1897), 187; Hogg at 28; Becker at 24; Beard, North and Price at 58; Keegan (2014) at 108.

24. John Henry Middleton. *The Remains of Ancient Rome*.Vol. 1. London: Adam and Charles Black (1892), 209.

25. Marucci at 325.

26. Richard Wunsch. *Sethianische verfluchungstafeln aus Rom*. Leipzig:B.G. Teubner (1898), 112.

27. Wunsch, *Sethianische verfluchungstafeln aus Rom*, 112-113.

28. Becker at 24.

which had been circulating around the city.[29] The city Tertullian references is likely Rome, based upon the work's dedication to the magistrates of Rome.[30]

Tertullian indicates that the representation he witnessed was produced by a contestant in the arena who ". . .displayed a picture with an inscription : "Onokoites, the god of the Christians."[31] Tertullian goes on in his description of the picture that was disseminated, stating that ". . .the figure had the ears of an ass, one foot was cloven, and it was dressed in a toga and carrying a book."[32] Certainly this description more than approximates the Alexamenos Graffiti in many of the significant details.

Tertullian speculates that the origin of the Roman belief that the Christian god had the characteristics of an ass came from none other than Cornelius Tacitus who, in the fifth book of his Histories, relayed an account of the Jewish War with references to the origin of their religious practices."[33] According to Tertullian, Tacitus states that the Jews were exiled from Egypt to the deserts of Arabia. Thirst afflicted the people there as the region was devoid of water. However, by tracking the movements of wild asses, the Jews were alerted to the presence of a spring. In gratitude for this, they deified the head of a wild ass as part of their worship.[34] Thus, according to Tertullian, Tacitus, understanding that Christianity originated from the Judaism, assumed that the Christians were " . . .devoted to the worship of this same image (i.e. a wild ass)." While certainly being in accord with scholars like Middleton and Wünsch that the practice of wild

---

29. Tertullian, *Apologeticus XVI..12* . Tertullian also makes a similar observation regarding pagan beliefs about an ass-headed Christian God in *Ad Nationes*, 1.14.

30. Tertullian, *Apologeticus* I.1; .

31. Tertullian, *Apologeticus* X VI. 12.

32. Tertullian, *Apologeticus* 51-52 ("Is erat auribus asininis, altero pede ungulatus, librum gestans et togatus"). It is uncertain where Tertullian saw the man in the areana with the portrayal similar to the Alexamenos Graffito. It could have been in his native North Africa or possoithe City of Rome.

33. Tertullian, *Apologeticus* XVI.1.

34. Tertullian, *Apologeticus* XVI.1-3.

ass worship had its origin prior to Christianity, Tertullian in no way interprets the depictions he has observed as being anything other than a polemic against the Christians. Becker categorically adopts this view and finds Tertullian's explanation as definitive.[35] Marucci, accepting Becker's arguments would add that, even if one grants the evidence that an ass-headed god was associated with Typhon-Seth on Roman curse tablets, these same tablets never portrayed the god as being crucified.[36]

On the whole, the testimony of Tertullian regarding a similar polemical representation positively identified as anti-Christian, coupled with Marucci and Becker's belief that the graffito's ass-headed god is a representation of Jesus of Nazareth, comports with other inscriptions in the Domus Gelatiana, which also in part make Christian references. Thus, it would appear that there is significant justification in rejecting those views of Middleton and Wünsch who posit sincere *adorare* of Gnostic deities in favor of those who would identify the ass-headed hominid as a polemical representation of Jesus of Nazareth. Modern Scholars likewise tend to agree with Marucci and Becker.[37]

With the probable identity of the ass-headed hominid established as Jesus of Nazareth rather than an Egyptian deity, it remains to be pointed out that, like Alexamenos, the ass-headed figure is wearing not a toga but rather the common tunic, a fact which is also loaded with polemic implication. While Roman representation of divinity from the first century on was diverse and could take many forms, the representation of a deity would always be proper and calculated to afford the god represented appropriate honor. This was because the Romans had, since the Republic, maintained that the success of the Roman State was in direct relation to the

35. Becker at 24.

36. Marucci at 325.

37. See John Keegan, *Grafitti in Antiquity* (2014), 108; Aliou Cissé Niang, Carolyn Osiek, Text, Image, and Christians in the Graeco-Roman World (2011), 244.

170 Kim Bowes. *Private Worship, Public Values and Religious Change in Late Antiquity.* (Cambridge: Cambridge University Press, 2008), 20-21.

constancy and propriety of the worship of Roman citizens.[38] Indeed, scrupulous piety was at the very heart of the concept of *religio* or "correctness" as to religious worship and". . .was regularly an aspect of a Roman's self-description." Thus, Valerius Maximus could claim in the first century that the gods indulged the Romans over their history since the Romans were so scrupulous in observing their cultic obligations.[39] Accordingly, the proper representation of a god would be one that would afford the god proper honors. Roman cult worked on the basis of orthopraxy, with the Roman gods and Roman citizens working hand in hand for the mutual benefit of all: in exchange for proper worship and veneration, the gods dispensed blessings upon the Roman State. Each part was the equal to the other. Proper veneration required that if the Roman gods were to be attired at all (and many, particularly gods, were not), would at least partially clothed in the best of attire: a Roman toga (or *stola* and *palla* if a goddess); Roman battle dress; or other attire congruent with and indicative of being worthy of the highest esteem. The ass-headed hominid, by contrast, is not attired in such a way as to suggest such a privileged status but is rather dressed as a commoner or provincial wearing an ordinary tunic. In so much as the figure is so attired, the suggestion is no doubt made by the creator of the graffiti that Alexamenos god is no god at all.

One last thing that deserves mention with regard to the ass headed hominid is the apparatus to which the figure is attached. It is universally agreed upon by scholars who have examined the graffito that the apparatus is a cross. This is apparent to the viewer in two ways. First, the central pole that bears the body of the ass-headed hominid is equipped with a foot rest, something one would associate with a person undergoing crucifixion, the rest not so much to offer relief as to prolong the misery of the process of crucifixion. Second, there appears on the figure's upper shoulder and upper torso below the shoulder marks which suggest the figure has suffered a wound. Again, this would be consistent with the

---

38.

39. Valerius Maximus. *Factorum et dictorum memorabilium*. 5.1.

over-all idea that the ass-headed figure, as portrayed, is intended
to be portrayed as being crucified.

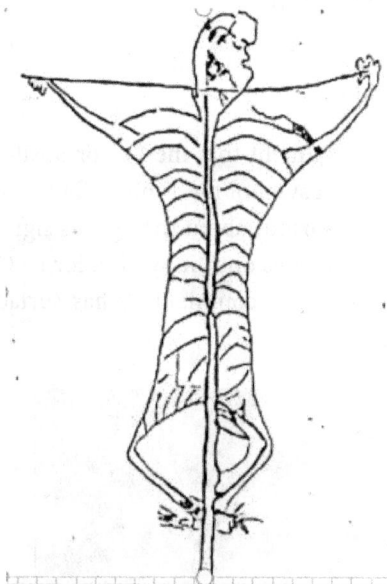

Rendering of Puteoli Crucifix
By Author

A further point of comparison to establish the crucifixion
of the ass-headed figure can be made with the so-called Puteoli
Crucifix discovered in 1959 in a roman shop (*taberna*) excavated
in the Italian town of Pozzuoli.[40] Dating from the Trajanic-Hadri-
anic era, the Crucifixion graffito was found among a number of
images, including the trident of a net fighter (*retiarius)*, a water organ, depictions of the god Pan, and nude women figures
dancing with torches in their hands.[41] As can be seen in Figure
16, there are notable similarities with the Alexamenos Graffito
which include the same T-shaped cross, the similar manner in
which the feet are attached to the central pole, and possible

40. John Granger Cook. *Crucifixion as Spectacle in Roman Campania*. Novum Testamentum 54, 1 (2012), 93.

41. Cook, *Crucifixion as Spectacle in Roman Campania*, 93.

evidence of wounding, in this case as demonstrated by the stripes which cover the crucified Puteoli figure, perhaps administered through the act of scourging.[42]

The "Y" or Upsilon

If one rejects the argument that the "Y" or upsilon figure is not to be interpreted as a symbol for Typhon-Seth worship, one still naturally would be curious about the figure's significance. Other than Wünsch, who singles out the symbol for its Gnostic significance, no other scholarly commentary has surfaced explaining its significance.

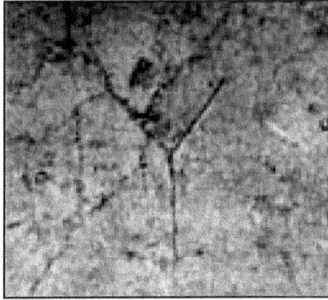

Y or Upsilon
Public Domain

This may not be altogether surprising given that some, if not all of the nineteenth century scholars who examined the graffiti, had the opportunity of seeing the surrounding context, that is, they saw the wall from which the Graffiti was extracted at a time when the wall was in some degree of preservation. To capture some idea of the context of the wall, it is instructive to reference Marucci who notes that ". . .[i]n the same room, on the same wall, to the right of the blasphemous graffito, there is this other inscription. HΔY/// ONAYTIΨ//// ATAΘΨN///AΨKAHΠΙΛOTOΨ//OΨKYΘHΨ."[43]

42. Cook, *Crucifixion as Spectacle in Roman Campania,* 93.

43. Horace Marucci. *The Roman Forum and the Palatine.* (Rome: Desclee

Horace Marucci translates this to read "Asclepiodote of the Sythian nation." He notes below this inscription is another, namely ΒΟΕΤΙΑ ΕΠΙΤΕΥ ΒΑΨΕΛΕΟΨ which he translates to "Help (comes) from (the) God King."[44] This later graffito is contained in a representation of a foot (see Figure 12, *supra*). Thus, rather than appearing in isolation, the Alexamenos Graffito appears within an overall matrix of numerous graffiti inscriptions. The "Y" figure, instead of being part of the Alexamenos array, may just as simply be a stray mark and in and of itself may mean nothing.

John Hogg observes that that the letter "Y" may be a pagan emblem representing human life.[45] Known as the *Samian* or the letter of Pythagorus, the letter was widely attested to in ancient literature and was said to graphically depict the two paths of life-the right branch being the path of virtue while the left branch being the path of vice.[46]

Lefebvre, 1906), 326.

44. Marucci, *Roman Forum and the Palatine*, 326.

45. Hogg at 37.

46. Hogg at 37. See also Perseus Satires III.56.

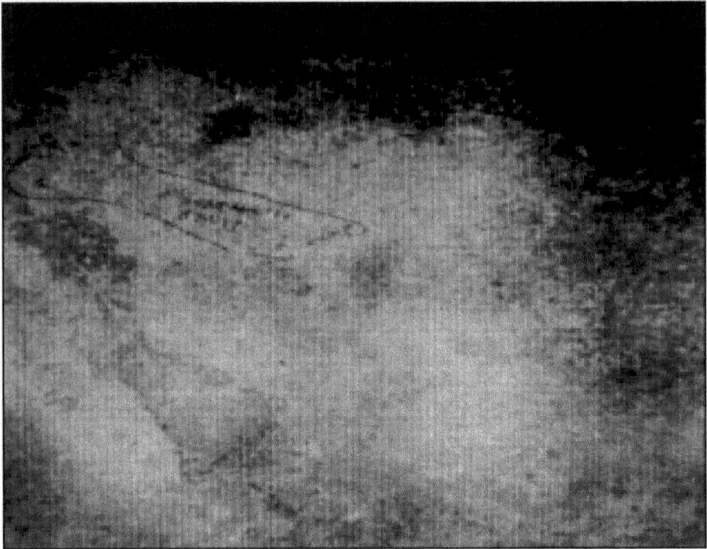

"Foot" Grafitto near Alexamenos Grafitto
Marucci/ Public Domain

While this is an appealing conjecture, a fact that mitigates against such an interpretation is that both branches of the Alexamenos "Y" are of even width while those of a *Samian* are uneven, the right branch representing virtue being narrower than the left, the virtuous path being the path less followed.[47] This differing width is not evident on the Alexamenos "Y" but may simply be the result of the instrument used to carve the Graffito, probably a nail.

Analysis of Graffiti near the Alexamenos Grafitto

In order to properly put the Alexamenos Graffito in its proper context, it is important to consider the graffiti proximate to the Alexamenos Graffito. As referenced earlier, this graffiti can help to provide insights about the identity of the author and the milieu in which the graffito was created. Unfortunately, in its present

47. Hogg at 87-88.

state of disrepair, the graffiti from the Domus Gelatiana have largely crumbled or faded away to oblivion. Fortunately, many of the authors cited in the work had first-hand knowledge of the graffiti cataloged what they saw, and translated the text. At present, a total of 369 graffiti have been identified and cataloged from the Pedagogium and the Domus Gelatiana[48]

What is immediately apparent when one reviews the multiple references to the graffiti in the Domus Gelatiana is the abundance of names who betray the geographical, occupational, or religious identities of those who passed through the Pedegogium and the Domus Gelatana. For example, two incriptions, *C. Emeleus Afer* and *Marianas Afer,* both contain the word *afer,* suggesting they were of African origin. Likewise, Asclepiodote's inscription, ΗΔΥ///ΟΝΑΥΤΙΨ//ΓΑΤΑΘΝ//// ΑΨΚΑΗΠΟΛΟΤΟΨΟΨΚΥΘΗΨΨ, readily identifies him being from the region of Scythia, which straddled both the Asian and European continents. Thus, it is abundantly clear that the occupants of the building were a cosmopolitan group who healed from multiple parts of the Roman Empire.

Secondarily, the several references to persons leaving the school is further evidence that the Domus Gelatiana and the Pedagogeum with which it was attached served in the capacity of an educational institution, This institution was possibly in the service of the Imperial Court as has been suggested or may have served some other educational function.

Next, a number of the graffiti make reference to particular occupations which were important to those who gathered at the Domus Gelatiana. Libanus is characterized as a Bishop, a strictly Christian occupation. Hilarus is described as a "our lord veteran soldier"

Finally, at least one of the graffiti makes possible reference to Christianity in a positive way. The phrase "ΒΟΕΤΙΑ ΕΠΙΤΕΥ ΒΑΨΕΛΕΟΨ" which Marucci translates as stating "Help comes from the god king" very much could be interpreted as a reference to Jesus of Nazareth who, as the purported Messiah, was politically

48. Oliver Larry Yarbrough, *Engaging the Passion: Perspectives on the Death of Jesus* (2015), 233.

viewed as King of the Jews but spiritually endorsed as being the spiritual savior who helps believers wash away their sins.

Dating the Alexamenos Graffito

Dating the Graffito, even given the significant accretion that has occurred in the domus Gelotiana, is not beyond the realm of possibility given the many clues which are available, both within the structure and through available texts. The conclusion reached by scholars Ferdinand Becker and John Hogg, which is adequately supported by the surviving material culture, is that the graffiti dates to the late second to early third century, perhaps created during the reign of Septimius Severus.[49] The justification given by Becker for such dating relates largely to Tertullian's reference in his *Apology* to similar tales of the Christians worshiping an ass-headed god.[50] The argument simply stated is that Tertullian's *Apology*, which references stories of Christian worship of an ass-headed god, approximates to the year 197, which in turn coincides with the reign of Septimius Severus (145-211 CE).[51] John Hogg, for his part, relates that the wall on which the graffiti was found was not only a part of Caligula's domus Gelotiana but also part of the Septizonium, a complex built by the Emperor Septimius Severus on the same site on the Palatine Hill, which, if correct, would confirm a date of the third century.[52] As mentioned before, Peter Keegan, when surveying the literature, found evidence of architectural elements which spanned the reigns of the Emperor Caligula to that of Septimius Severus.[53]

---

49. Becker at 33-35; John Hogg. *On a Profane Stylograph of the Crucifixion at Rome*. Transactions of the Royal Society of Literature of the United Kingdom, IX (1870), 27-28.

50. Becker at 33.

51. Henry Chadwick. *The Early Church*. London: Penguin Books (1957), 216-217.

52. Hogg at 27-28.

53. Peter Keegan (2014) at 108.

Finally, John Middleton notes that the Circus Maximus, the large stadium immediately to the south of the Domus Augusta, is characterized by brick facings which carry bricks stamps which have connections to the Flavian Dynasty (69-96 CE) as well as stamps which betray their origin during the reign of Hadrian (127-138 CE).[54] Taking the evidence provided by Tertullian in conjunction with the architectural evidence, an educated guess could date the Alexamenos Graffito to a period between the late first century to the second decade of the third century, or roughly between 69-211 CE.

With this being said, one source of information narrows the time frame considerably. Esther Van Deman, writing a monograph for the British School at Rome in 1916, undertook an architectural survey not only of the buildings surrounding the Domus Gelatiana and the Pedogaogium but also these very buildings as well.[55] Van Deman concluded from brickstamps and architectural continuity that the Pedagogium dated from the Flavian reign of Domition or that of Hadrian, while the date of the Domus Gelatiana was clearly from the Severan era, based on the buildings general construction and its use of "broken bipedales for the brick facing-a type of facing found of no dated monuments earlier than those of the Severans and especially characteristic of their work."[56]

Thus, the probable date of the Alexamenos Graffito which was found in the Domus Gelatiano must correspond to the Severan era (193-211 CE). This determination is based not only on the particular brick facing employed in the structure characteristic of the Severan Dynasty but also the corresponding narrative of Tertullian who makes his observations of a similar graffito during the same time period.

---

54. Middleton at 126.

55. Esther B. Van Deman, *Appendix: On the Date of the Brickwork of the House in the Vie De Cerchi and of the Surrounding Buildings.* Papers of the British School at Rome. Vol. VIII. London: Macmillan and Co. 1916., 102-103.

56. Van Deman, *Appendix: On the Date of the Brickwork,* 103.

CHAPTER SEVEN

Conclusion

The Historical Significance of
the Alexamenos Graffito

BUILDINGS RECORD THE ATTITUDES and values of those who live
in them. Whether through construction, ornamentation or inscriptions within the building made by the occupants or passers-
by, an archeologist or historian looking at a historic building can
gather quite a bit about the buildings occupants by what is found
inside.[1] This has been no less true for the Pedagogium and the
Domus Gelatiana.

While taking probably less than a few moments to create,
the Alexamenos Graffito can provide significant insights into the
persons who dwelled within the walls of these structures, their
attitudes toward others, and a partial view of the environment
in which these persons lived. These insights have the potential
to be multifaceted and historically significant. However, there is
a great deal that can't be known and a equal body of knowledge
that depends on speculation.

1. Peter Keegan, "Reading the 'Pages' of the Domus Caesarius; Pueri Delicati, Slave Education, and the Grafitti of the Pedagogium" in Roman Slavery
and Roman Material Culture. Ed. Michele George. Toronto: University of Toronto Press (2013), 70.

In the realm of what can likely be known, the Alexamenos Graffito was in all probability created in the nearly twenty years that straddled both the second and third centuries of the Common Era. This was a time when Christianity was beginning to emerge as a tangible influence among the citizenry of the Roman Empire. It was also the period of the great Christian apologists like Tertullian and Municius Felix and pagan protagonists like Celsus who rhetorically dueled in the more rarefied environment of public opinion. That the presence and activities of Christians had ceased to go unnoticed is evident on the highest levels, where the Emperor Trajan and his Bythnian Governor Pliny carried on protracted communication about how the Christians were to be treated and whether they should be allowed to continue their activities which appeared so at variance with the established Roman State Religion.

Likewise, it is fairly clear from the content of the Alexamenos Graffito that the author of the Graffito was a literate individual, with a knowledge of Greek and some familiarity with Judaism and its offshoot, Christianity. This person was not the only one with such knowledge. The other graffiti on the walls demonstrate that in addition to the author of the Graffito, others were present who had knowledge of Christianity, with at least one references to the hierarchy of the church. As to Alexamenos, it is reasonably probable that he was of Greek extract. John Hogg notes that the name is a typical name found among the Greeks and has some notoriety, Livy having mentioned it in his works.[2]

Given the references among the graffiti which suggest that the Pedagogium was a school, it seems probable that the author of the Alexamenos Graffito may have been in the process of receiving an education there. If this is correct, a few things can likewise be deduced. First, the very fact that the author of the graffito was at a formal educational institution very likely means that the individual was male. As Paul Veyne has observed with regard to Roman education, only "young boys attended school" in the formal sense, while education for girls was either nonexistent or presided

2. Hogg at 34.

over by private tutors in the home.[3] Moreover, it is not too much of a conjecture to suggest that the author and those persons who occupied the Pedagogium and Domus Gelatiana were well off. Schools of the era were not public in any modern sense with the costs absorbed by the state. Rather, schools were private affairs, with lesser institutions taking up lessons in outdoors in public spaces and sidewalks while more elaborate schools met indoors. As a school that was indoors, it would be more likely that those students in attendance were well off to enable them to afford the fees.[4] This view is reinforced by another clue which also suggests that the author was of higher financial standing. This is demonstrated by the author of the Alexamenos Graffito's apparant antipathy toward the Christian religion which he expresses through his demeaning depiction of both Alexamenos, who is portrayed as a backward person of the lower class with ill-formed manners, as well as Alexamenos' god, whom he likewise portrays as half-animal, half man, and crucified as only a person who was not a Roman citizen could be, and further like Alexamenos, a person who dresses as though he were a member of the lower classes. That such an opinion would be expressed, even indirectly, that Christianity is a religious practice found among the lower orders of society and by persons who were not Romans suggests that perhaps the author of the Grafitto was not only a Roman citizen but also also considered himself to be of higher standing and beyond the lower class superstitions of the Christians.

The type of education being provided by the Pedagogium can also be hinted at by the content of the Graffito. The author's use of Greek rather than Latin can mean several things. It may mean that the author was of eastern extract and his knowledge of the language was natural. So too it is possible that the author had been privately tutored in the language at home, probably by a slave as was commonplace, and thus was at least marginally fluent in the language. But another possibility exists that the student was being

---

3. Paul Veyne, "The Roman Empire" in *A History of Private Life*. Ed. Paul Veyne (1987), 19-20.

4. Veyne, "Roman Empire," 19.

taught Greek at the Pedagogium. Regarding this latter possibility, it should be pointed out that Roman education was generally divided into three phases. The first was presided over by a *magister* or *litterator* who taught the students under his care basic literacy, grammar, and arithmetic, presumably in the vernacular Latin.[5] However, at the next educational level, students were taught by a *grammaticus*, who enabled the student to embellish his writing style and introduced the student to the Greek language if they had not thus far been exposed to it.[6] Boys who studied under a *grammaticus* were at least ten or eleven years of age.[7] While certainly the words used by the author may have already have been part of his lingual catalogue but it is possible that this person ability to taunt Alexamenos came from study in the classroom.

As to other things that can be gleaned from a study of the Graffito, it should next be observed that their content nearly reaffirm the North African Tertullian's observations of the similar characterizations of the Christian god. Given that we know that some of the students of the Pedagogium came from the African continent, perhaps such stories made their way to Rome through these foreigners and into the ears of the author of the Alexamenos Graffito. Perhaps similar happenings were occurring on the Italian Peninsula. Regardless of the inspiration, however, a reasonable inference can be made that the Pegagogium was a highly cosmopolitan gathering of individuals and likely that the persons within the school had a significant grasp of emerging social trends. This is not altogether surprising since the purpose of Roman education beyond the elementary school years was to confer prestige upon students, by "embellishing their minds" by cultivation with literature and mythology.[8] It would not be a stretch to consider that the mythology of other lands and peoples might make its way into educational discussions or at worst, into school

5. Jo-Ann Shelton, *As the Romans Did*. Oxford: Oxford University Press (1988), 10–107.

6. Shelton, *As the Romans Did,* 107.

7. Shelton, *As the Romans Did,* 107.

8. Veyne, "Roman Empire," 20.

gossip. Furthermore, such a dispersion of epigraphic "ideas" has been observed in other contexts as well. For instance, Peter Keegan has noted that a particular graffito found in Pompeii, to wit, "ADMIROR O PARIENS TE NON CECIDISSE RVINIS QVI TOT SCRIPTORVM TAEDIA SVSTINEAS" which Keegan translates as "I am amazed, O wall, that you have not fallen in ruins, you who support the tediousness of so many writers" has been found reproduced in Greek in areas considerably removed from Pompeii, with inscriptions noted as well as the Palatine.[9]

Having considered some of the implications on a more mundane level, it is important to also consider the Graffito for its higher, more societal implications. Most graffiti in antiquity, like the graffiti of today, were fairly pedestrian and one-dimensional. They typically relate to everyday wants and wishes, loves and hatreds. Usually, they point of the graffito was to memorialize and celebrate the existence of the author, to tell the world and those who come after that they were at a certain place at a certain time.

9. Peter Keegan, Texting Rome: Grafitti as Speech Act and Cultural Discourse. Ancient Grafitti in Context Workshop (Leicester University November 8, 2008), 19-20.

Contemporary Grafitto.
Inverness, UK/ Photo by Author

Rare is the occasion when a graffito conveys any more of a substantive message though it is certainly true that the same exists. The Alexamenos Graffito transcends the mundane and, whether intentionally or not, addresses a number of questions which were at the center of the cultural debate about the sacred in the second and third centuries of the Common Era. The first of these issues is the radical monotheism of the Christians and the Jews versus the widespread polytheism of the Roman people.

As discussed earlier, the Roman people and the Roman State placed a premium on their veneration of a diverse pantheon of gods. While not altogether alien from Roman cult, monotheism was rarely promoted prior to the later third and early fourth centuries. The monotheistic cult of the Emperor Bassianus (or Elagabalus), *deus Sol Invictus,* is one notable exception.[10] A short lived affair, the Severan Emperor Bassianus promoted this cult whose central image was a conical black stone.[11] It died with Bassianus' assassination, the impetus being not only revolt against the emperor, who behavior in a manner that was on par with Nero and Calligula, but also because the cult worship he promoted was considered suspect.[12]

Considering the Alexamenos Graffito, the obvious scorn manifested by the author of the Graffito toward Alexameno's god was not his alone but was rather commonly held, as we learn from Tertullian, whose *Apology* references a catalogue of complaints about Christianity, including against the religion's Christian monotheism which excludes veneration and worship of any god but the God of the Hebrews.[13]

The second substantive issue raised by the author of the Graffito is the nature of the gods. To the Romans, the gods were wholly divine even if they behaved as humans or had what would be considered human attributes. One way this divine nature manifested itself was through the gods' immortality.[14] Still another was through the gods' immunity to concerns of the world.[15] Still another was the gods the way they confined their activities to their proper sacred sphere, rejecting and avoiding the sphere of the profane.[16] In sum, the gods generally stayed in their world and humans in theirs, anything less was viewed either as condescension by the gods or hubris by mortals. Celsus highlights this point in his *Alēthēs logos* ("On the True Doctrine") where he criticizes

10. Arthur E.R. Boak, *History of Rome to 565 A.D 4d.* (1955), 337

11. Boak *History of Rome to 565 A.D 4d.* 337.

12. Boak *History of Rome to 565 A.D 4d.* 337.

13. Tertullian, *Apology* 10.1

14. Lucretius, *De Rerum Natura* 3:13-24

15. Lucretius, *De Rerum Natura* 3:23-24.

16. Roepke at 80.

Christians for their belief in the humanity of Jesus of Nazareth which he felt was below the dignity of a god.[17] Likewise, the author of the Graffito makes such a criticism, though less directly, through his portrayal of Alexamenos' god as anything but a god but rather only a rube, fitted with the clothing of a common person; as less than a human, portraying the god as half-ass, half man; and unworthy of the highest consideration as either a person of either high status or a Roman citizen, the god notably being crucified as only a non-Roman citizen could be.

Finally, another substantive issue raised by the Alexamenos Graffito is the portrayal of crucifixion in the third century. Few representations of crucifixion exist from this era and the Alexamenos Graffito provides a rare representation, among few others, of the mechanical aspects of crucifixion.[18] Among those representations that remain include the afore-mentioned Puteoli Crucifix; a third century representation of a crucifix found at the Palace of the Caesars in the mid-nineteenth century[19]; and a third century gem bearing the image of a crucifixion.[20] Interestingly, both the Puteoli Crucifix and the crucifix found at the Palace of the Caesars share with the Alexamenos Graffito the same "T" shaped cross.[21] With so few exemplars remaining, the Alexamenos Graffito provides contemporary scholars with one of the few views available of Roman crucifixion methods from which to analyze this method of punishment utilized by the Romans.

With all these considerations in play, it is clear that the Alexamenos Graffito is an important artifact of second to third century Roman material culture. It not only reflects the then existing antipathy toward Christians but also reveals a great deal about the author as well as those who had a presence at the Pedagogium and the Domus Gelatiana. Rather than merely being a "blasphemous

17. Celsus, *On the True Doctrine*. Trans. R. Joseph Hoffman (1987), 66-67

18. Hogg at 29-30.

19. Hogg at 30.

20. C. Smith . "The Crucifixion on a Greek Gem." *The Annual of the British School at Athens.* 1897;3:201-206.

21. Hogg at 30.

representation of Christ" the Graffito is a fully articulated representation by an ordinary individual of the arguments that were
then prevalent at the highest levels of Roman society. Its repetition
of rhetoric that was being advanced across the Mediterranean is
a strong anecdote of the culture war that was being waged in the
late Seond to early Third Centuries of the Common Era, a cultural
war which would eventually erupt in violence, the persecution of
Christians across the empire, but also the dissolution of the ancient
Roman temples and the conversion of an emperor to the cause that
Alexamenos was aligned to so many decades before.

APPENDIX I

Chronology of Approximate Key Dates in Ancient Roman and Christian History

27 BCE Octavian assumes title of Augustus.

7 CE Jesus of Nazareth born

14 CE Augustus dies. Succeeded by Tiberius.

30 CE Crucifixion of Jesus of Nazareth.

37 CE Tiberius dies. Succeeded by Gaius (Caligula).

41 CE Gaius assassinated. Succeeded by Claudius.

54 CE Claudius dies. Succeeded by Nero.

64 CE Great fire at Rome.

69 CE Nero commits suicide. Vespasian becomes emperor.

70 CE Sack of Jerusalem.

81 CE Domitian becomes emperor.

96 CE Domitian assassinated. Nerva becomes emperor.

98 CE Trajan becomes emperor.

117 CE Trajan dies.

155 CE Tertullian born.

160 CE Justin Martyr writes *Dialogue with Trypho the Jew.*

161 CE Marcus Aurelius becomes emperor.

177 CE Celsus writes *The True Doctrine* against Christianity.

180 CE Marcus Aurelius dies.

193 CE Septimius Severus becomes emperor.

197 CE Tertullian writes *Apologeticus.*

202 CE Perpetua and Felicitas martyred in Carthage.

211 CE Septimius Severus dies.

240 CE Tertullian dies.

284 CE Diocletion becomes emperor.

302 CE Great persecution of Christians begins.

306 CE Constantine becomes emperor.

Map of City of Rome Around the Third Century CE

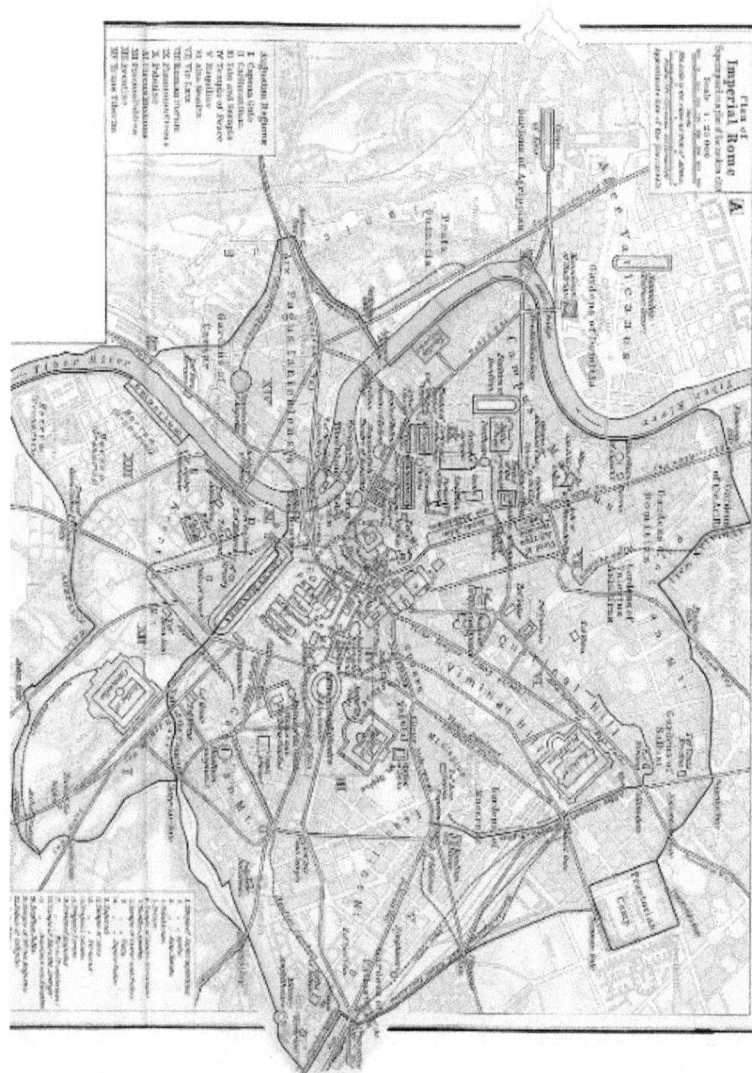

APPENDIX III

Select Grafitti from the Pedagogicum and Domus Gelatiana

Latin Graffiti

Grafitto	Source	Translation
Corinthus exit de Paedagogio	Lanciani/ Middleton	Corinthus leaves the school.
Marianus afer exit de pedagogio	Lanciani/ Middleton	Marianus (the African) leaves the school.
Et Proderit Tibi Labora Aselle Quomodo Ego Laboravi	*Lanciani*/ Middleton	Work, O Ass as I have labored and you have profited.
Verna domini nostril	Becker	Verna our master
Libanus Episcopus	Becker	Libanus (the) Bishop
Hilarus M(iles) V(eteranus) D(omini) N(ostri)	Middleton	Hilarus our lord veteran soldier
C Emeleus Afer	Middleton	C. Emeleus (the African)

APPENDIX III: SELECT GRAFITTI

Grafitto	Source	Translation
Doryphorus	Middleton	Doryphorus (cognomen
Asiaticus	Middleton	Asiaticus (cognomen)
Rogatus	Middleton	Rogatus (cognomen)
Paramithius	Lanciani	Paramithius (cognomen)
Gemellys	Lanciani	Gemellys (cognomen)
Incenus	Lanciani	Incenus (cognomen)
Felicis	Middleton	Felicis (cognomen)

Greek Grafitti

Grafitto	Source	Translation
HΔY/// ONAYTIC///	Marucci	Asclepiodote of the Sythian nation
BOETIA EΠITEY BACIΛEOC	Marucci	Help comes from the god king.
AKINΘOC	Middleton	AKINΘOC (cognomen)

Bibliography

All Latin and Greek classical references are made to the standard addition of the Loeb Classical Library, unless otherwise noted.

Aubert, J.J. "A Double Standard in Roman Criminal Law?." In *Speculum Iuris: Roman Law as a Reflection of Social and Economic Life in Antiquity*. Edited by J.-J. Aubert and B. Sirks. Ann Arbor: University of Michigan, 2002.

Asad, Talal. "Anthropological Conceptions of Religion: Reflections on Geertz," *Man, New Series* 18(2) (1983): 237-259.

Beard, Mary, John North and Simon Price. *Religions of Rome*. Vol.1 and 2. Cambridge: Cambridge University Press,1998.

Becker, Ferdinand. *Das Spott-Crucifix der römischen Kaiserpaläste aus dem Anfange des dritten Jahrhunderts*. Breslau: Max Malser, 1866.

Benario, H.W.. *Rome of the Severi*. Paris: Latomis. T. 17, Fasc. 4. October-December, 1958.

Benko, Stephen. *Pagan Rome and the Early Christians*. Bloomington, Indiana: Indiana University Press, 1986.

Birchman, Robert. *Porphyry: Against the Christians*. Boston: Brill, 2005.

Boak, Arthur E.R., *A History of Rome*. New York:The McMillan Company, 1955.

Bodel, John. *Cicero's Minerva, Penates, and the Mother of the Lares: An Outline of of Roman Domestic Religion* in *Household and Family Religion in Antiquity*. Edited by John Bodel and Saul M. Olyan. Oxford: Blackwell, 2008.

Boerthius, Axel, *Etruscan and Early Roman Architecture*. London: Penguin, 1987.

Bowes, Kim. *Private Worship, Public Values and Religious Change in Late Antiquity*. Cambridge: Cambridge University Press, 2008.

Brown, Peter. *The World of Late Antiquity*. London: Thames and Hudson, 1971.

———. "Late Antiquity" in *A History of Private Life*. Edited by Paul Veyne. Cambridge: Belknap 1987, 235-297.

Celsus. *On the True Doctrine*. Translated by R. Joseph Hoffman. Oxford: Oxford University Press,1987.

Chadwick, Henry. *The Early Church*. London: Penguin Books, 1993.

Claridge, Amanda. *Oxford Archeological Guides.* Rome: Oxford University Press, 1998.

Cook, John Granger. "Crucifixion as a Spectacle in Roman Campania." *Novum Testamentum* 54 (2012): 84.

de Coulanges, Fustel, *The Ancient City* (Garden City, New York: Doubleday Anchor, 1864.

Cowell, F.R. *Life in Ancient Rome.* New York: Capricorn, 1975.

Cumont, Francis, *Oriental Religions in Roman Paganism.* Translated by Grant Showerman. New York: Dover, 1956.

Crosson, John Dominic and Jonathan L. Reed. *In Search of Paul.* New York: HarperSanFrancisco, 2004.

Dill, Samuel *Roman Society from Nero to Marcus Aurelius.* New York: Meridian, 1954.

Dio Cassius, "Epitome", in *The New Eusebius*, ed. J. Stevenson. London: SPCK, 1978.

Dunn, Daisy. *The Shadow of Vesuvius: A Life of Pliny.* London: Norton, 2019.

Durkheim, Emile. *The Elementary Forms of Religious Life.* Translated by Joseph Ward Swain. New York: Freepress/MacMillan, 1915.

Embleton, Ronald and Frank Graham. *Hadrian's Wall.* New York: Dorset, 1984.

Eusebius, *The History of the Church.* Translated by G.A. Williamson. London: Penguin, 1989.

Farrar, F.W. *The Early Days of Christianity.* London: Cassell and Co. Ltd., 1884.

Favro, Dian "Making Rome a World City" in *The Cambridge Companion to the Age of Augustus.* Edited by Karl Galinsky. Cambridge: Cambridge University Press, 2005: 240-249.

Fentress, Elizabeth. "Romanizing the Berbers," *Past & Present.* No. 190. (Feb. 2006): 3-33.

Finegan, Jack. *The Archeology of the New Testament.* Princeton, New Jersey: Princeton University Press, 1992.

Frazer, James George, The *Golden Bough.* New York: Collier/Macmillan, 1922.

Geertz, Clifford. *The Interpretation of Cultures.* San Francisco: Basic Books, 1973.

Grant, Frederick C., Editor, *Ancient Roman Religion.* New York: Liberal Arts Press (1957).

Grant, Michael. *The Etruscans.* New York: Quality Paperbacks, 1997.

Harley, Felicity. "Crucifixion in Roman Antiquity: The State of the Field," *Journal of Early Christian Studies,* 27. 2 (Summer 2019): 303-323.

Harnack, Adolf, *The Mission and Expansion of Christianity.* Translated by James Moffatt. New York: Harper Torchbooks, 1961.

Hogg, John. "On a Profane Stylograph of the Crucifixion at Rome." in *Transactions of the Royal Society of Literature of the United Kingdom.* IX 1870: 27-28.

Keegan, Peter. "Roman Slavery and Roman Material Culture". Conference Paper in *The Sixth E. T. Salmon Conference in Roman Studies: Roman Slavery and Roman Material Culture.* Hamilton, Ontario: McMaster University. September 28-29, 2007.

Keegan, Peter. "Texting Rome: Grafitti as Speech Act and Cultural Discourse," in *Ancient Grafitti in Context Workshop*. Leicester University (November 8, 2008), 19-20.

———. "Reading the 'Pages' of the Domus Caesarius; Pueri Delicati, Slave Education, and the Grafitti of the Pedagogium," in *Roman Slavery and Roman Material Culture*. Edited by Michele George. Toronto: University of Toronto Press 2013.

Keppie, Lawrence, *The Making of the Roman Army*. New York: Barnes and Noble, 1984.

Lanciani, Rudolfo Amedeo. *Ancient Rome in Light of Recent Discoveries*. Boston: Houghton Mifflin,1889.

———. *The Ruins and Excavations of the Palatine: A Companion Book for Students and Travelers*. Boston: Houghton Mifflin, 1897.

———. *Ruins and Excavations of Ancient Rome*. Boston and New York: Houghton, Mifflin, 1897.

Leibner, Ashley, "The Anthropology of Religion: Historical and Contemporary Trends," in *Macmillan Handbooks on Religion: Historical Consciousness and the Social Sciences*. Edited by William B. Parsons. London: Palgrave Macmillan, 2016.

MacCulloch, Diarmaid. *Christianity: The First Three Thousand Years*. New York: Viking, 2009.

Mackay, Christopher S., *Ancient Rome*. Cambridge: Cambridge University Press, 2004.

Marti, Berthe M.."*Proskynesis and Adorare*," *Language*. 12, no. 4 (Oct.-Dec. 1936).

Marucci, Horace. *The Roman Forum and the Palatine According to the Latest Discoveries*. Rome: Desclee Lefebvre, 1906.

Mattingly, David. *An Imperial Possession: Britain and the Roman Empire*. London: Penguin, 2007.

Meeks, Wayne A. *The First Urban Christians*. New Haven: Yale University Press, 1983.

Meggitt, Justin. "Did Magic Matter? The Saliency of Magic in the Early Roman Empire," *Journal of Ancient History*, Vol. 1, Issue 2 (2013): 173-174.

Merrill, Elmer Truesdell, "The Attitude of Ancient Rome Toward Religion and Religious Cults," *The Classical Journal*. Vol. 15. No 4. (January 1920): 196-215.

Middleton, John Henry. *Ancient Rome in 1888*. Edinburgh: Adam and Charles Black, 1888.

Middleton, John Henry. *The Remains of Ancient Rome*. Vol. 1. London: Adam and Charles Black, 1892.

Miller, J. Lane, Harper's Bible Dictionary. New York: Harper and Brothers, 1961.

Ministero per i Beni e le Attivita Culturali sopintendenza Archeologica de Roma at 3-4.

Minucius Felix. *Octavius*. Translated by Rudolph Arbesmann. Washington:Catholic University of America Press, 1950.

Moynihan, Brian. *The Faith*. New York: Doubleday, 2002.

Ogilvie, R. M., *The Romans and Their Gods in the Age of Augustus*. New York: Norton, 1969.

Origen, *Contra Celsum*. Translated by Henry Chadwick. Cambridge: Cambridge University Press, 1953.

Eusebius Pamphilius. "Church History" in *Nicene and Post Nicene Fathers*. Ed. Philip Schaff. (Grand Rapids, Michigan: Wm. B. Erdmans 1890), V. I-VII

Petronius, *The Satyricon*. Translated by J.P. Sullivan. London: Penguin, 1986.

Placher, William C., *A History of Christian Theology*. Louisville, KY: Westminster John Knox, 1983.

Pliny, Epp. X. in *The New Eusebius*, ed. J. Stevenson. London: SPCK, 1978.

Potter, David S., "Roman Religion: Ideas and Action" in *Life, Death, and Entertainment in the Roman Empire*, ed. D.S. Potter and D.J. Mattingly. Ann Arbor: University of Michigan Press, 1999.

Rupke, Jorg. *Religion of the Romans*. Cambridge: Polity Press, 2007.

Scarre, Chris, *Historical Atlas of Ancient Rome*. London: Penguin,1995.

Schaff, Philip, *Nicene and Anti-Nicene Fathers*, Edinborough, 1890.

Schulz, Celia E., "The Romans and Ritual Murder" *Journal of the American Academy of Religion* 78. 2 (June 2010): 516-541.

Smith, C. "The Crucifixion on a Greek Gem" in *Annual of the British Schol at Athens*, 1897: 3:201–206.

Suetonius, "Nero" and "Caligula" in *The Twelve Caesars*. Translated by Robert Graves. London: Penguin, 1957.

Tacitus, *The Complete Works of Tacitus*. Translated by Alfred John Church and William Jackson Brodribb. New York: The Modern Library, 1942.

Taylor, L. Ross Taylor, *The Cults of Ostia*. Chicago: Ares Publishing, 1913.

Tertullian, *Apology*. Translated by Sister Emily Joseph Daly. Washington: Catholic University of America Press, 1950.

Turcan, Robert, *The Cults of the Roman Empire*. Translated by Antonia Nevill. Oxford: Blackwell, 1992.

Uden, James "The Margins of Satire: Suetonius, Satura, and Scholarly Outsiders in Ancient Rome" *American Journal of Philology* 141. 4 (Winter 2020): 575-601.

Valerius Maximus, *Memorable Sayings and Doings*.Vol. I. Translated by D.R. Shakelton Bailey. Cambridge: Harvard University Press, 2000.

Van Deman, Esther. "On the Date of the Brickwork on the house in the Via De Cerchi and of the Surrounding Buildings." Appendix attached to Mrs. Arthur Strong. In *The Fragments of Ancient Wall Paintings in Rome. II. The House of the Via de Cerchi. Papers of the British School at Rome* 8. 4. (1916): 102-103.

Von Mach, Edmund. *University Prints: Series A: Greek and Roman Sculpture*. Boston: The University Prints, 1916.

Wallace-Hadrill, Andrew, *Mutatas Formas: The Augustan Transformation of Roman Knowledge* in *The Cambridge Companion to the Age of Augustus*. Cambridge: Cambridge University Press 2005: 77.

Ward-Perkins, J.B., *Roman Imperial Architecture*. London: Penguin, 1989.

Warrior, Valerie M. *Roman Religion: A Sourcebook*. Newburyport, Massachusetts: Focus, 2002.

White, L. Michael, *Scripting Jesus*. New York: HarperOne, 2010.

Wilken, Robert L., *The Christians as the Romans Saw Them*. New Haven: Yale University Press, 1984.

Woolf, Greg, "Beyond Romans and Natives," *World Archaeology* 28 (3) (1995): 339-350.

Woolf, Greg, *Rome: An Empire's Story*. Oxford: Oxford University Press, 2012.

Wunsch, Richard. *Sethianische verfluchungstafeln aus Rom*. Leipzig:B.G. Teubner, 1898.

Wulf-Rheidt, Ulrick "The Palaces of the Roman Emperor's on Palatine in Rome" in *The Emperor's House*. ed Michael Featherstone, et. al. Berlin: de Gruyter 2015, 6.

Wünsch, Richard. *Sethianische verfluchungstafeln aus Rom*. Leipzig: B.G. Teubner,1898.

Yarbrough, Oliver Larry. *Engaging the Passion: Perspectives on the Death of Jesus*. Minneapolis: Fortress, 2015.